10 Steps to Create a Trauma-Informed Resilient School

Caelan Soma, PsyD, LMSW
Derek Allen, MA, ACTP

STARR
COMMONWEALTH

ISBN: 1-931310-63-7
© 2017, Revised May 2021

Starr Commonwealth
13725 Starr Commonwealth Road, Albion, Michigan 49224

www.starr.org

www.starr.org

ABOUT THE AUTHORS

Dr. Caelan Soma, PsyD, LMSW, Starr Commonwealth's Chief Clinical Officer, provides oversight for all clinical operations and research at Starr Commonwealth.

Dr. Soma provides trauma assessment and trauma-informed, resilience-focused intervention for youth utilizing evidence-based practices, including Starr's SITCAP® model programs.

She has been involved in helping with the aftermath of disasters such as Sandy Hook, Hurricanes Katrina and Rita, and others. She has authored several books, including her most recent, *Healing the Experience of Trauma: A Path to Resilience.*

She is an internationally acclaimed speaker and trainer, and is the instructor for many Starr courses, including *Children of Trauma and Resilience* and *Structured Sensory Interventions II.* She received her doctorate in clinical psychology at California Southern University, where she received the 2013 CalSouthern President's Award.

Derek Allen, MA, ACTP, Starr Commonwealth's Executive Vice President and Chief Operating Officer, provides administrative leadership to all Starr programs as well as leads the organization's business development efforts. Programs include residential treatment, community-based behavioral health services, the resilient schools and communities initiative, and professional training and coaching.

He also serves as a Senior Consultant for Starr's professional training and coaching arm. In this role, Derek works with partners of Starr Commonwealth to develop, launch, and sustain programs leading to systemic change in schools and community as it relates to trauma-informed, resilience-focused care and practices.

Finally, Derek provides "thought-leadership" to the Starr organization in the areas of strength-based approaches in education and treatment and building resilience in children and families. Derek is currently pursuing a doctoral degree from The Chicago School of Professional Psychology.

Starr Professional Training and Coaching emerges from the vision that : knowledge + empowerment = impact.

Starr provides guidance and expertise to educators, clinicians, and many others who care for children from around the world in the form of research, publications, e-learning courses, in-person trainings, conferences and events, professional certifications, as well as school/organization-wide accreditation. These products and services have been developed through our three key legacy training programs: The National Institute for Trauma and Loss in Children (TLC), Reclaiming Youth International (RYI), and Glasswing (GW).

www.starr.org

TABLE OF CONTENTS

Introduction

This resource provides all school professionals with an understanding of the science of childhood trauma and resilience, and specifically how both impact learning and behavior. Included are ten concrete steps to guide both the creation and implementation of a trauma-informed, resilient school.

> For children who have experienced trauma, learning can be a real struggle. But once trauma is identified as the root of behavior, educators can adapt their approach to help kids cope at school.

Childhood trauma refers to any experience in a child's life that leaves them feeling hopeless, helpless and stuck, or fearing for their life, safety, or survival — or for the life, safety, or survival of a loved one. Examples include neglect, physical and sexual abuse, domestic violence, natural disasters, incarceration of a loved one, accidents, and war. Childhood trauma also comes in the form of toxic stress experiences such as poverty, homelessness, chronic bullying, or living with parents, caregivers, or siblings who have mental and physical health challenges or are struggling with addiction.

SAMHSA's (2014) concept of trauma is defined as follows:

Individual trauma results from an event, series of events, or set of circumstances experienced by an individual as physically or emotionally harmful or life-threatening and having lasting adverse effects on the individual's functioning and mental, physical, social, emotional, or spiritual well-being (p. 7, 2014).

The definition is expanded upon through the use of the three "E's" of trauma: event, experience, and effect.

THE EVENT

The event may be a single occurrence or be repeated over time, and may include actual or extreme threat of harm. While there are many events that may be potentially traumatizing, we can't assume that exposure to them always leads to post-traumatic stress symptoms and reactions. There are children exposed to similar events who will respond very differently from one another. Why is this? The answers lies in the experience and the child's resilience (which is the entire focus of Step 1 in this book.)

THE EXPERIENCE

It is the experience or perception of the event by the child that determines whether it is a traumatic event – to them. For example, we may view parent incarceration as a potentially traumatizing event. However, if the child of that parent experiences this event as one that provides them with relief, it is not then traumatic.

CASE EXAMPLE: MEGAN

Megan was referred when she was in 4th grade by her school principal, who found out that Megan's father was recently incarcerated.Megan was having difficulty paying attention in class and seemed to be withdrawing from her peers. Upon meeting Megan, she was asked to tell a little bit about herself. She readily explained that she just moved in with her grandfather because her father was "locked up." She went on quickly to say, "I am so happy my daddy is in jail – now we don't have to worry about him getting killed on the streets by the other gang." Later, during the sessions, it was learned that Megan's grandfather suffered from diabetes and had recently started dialysis. When asked about her biggest worry she said, "If my grand-daddy dies, my Mom and I will be homeless."

This example shows us how adults may assume a specific event as traumatic, when in fact an alternate experience is causing a child's stress response. We can't assume that certain events are traumatic until we understand how a child experiences that event. We must consider this as well for events that may seem "trivial." For example, the sky begins to turn dark and a child panics. This is common for any child who experienced a natural disaster such as a flood or hurricane.

The lessons we must learn about the experience are:

1. Never assume something small **isn't** traumatizing
2. Never assume something that seems awful **is** traumatizing
3. The child's perception of the event is **their** experience – not our experience.

THE EFFECT

The experience then influences the effect of the event, over the short to long term. A short term acute stress response is common and should be normalized following overwhelming events. When a child has a prolonged and exaggerated stress response to the experience of any event, that is when we will observe post-traumatic stress symptoms and reactions.

While specific events are important to identify, we must not forget how those events are experienced and for how long a child endures that experience or a combination of experiences. In many cases there is not just one thing that has happened but a constant experience of stress related to multiple exposures. As we focus on critical events that receive the attention of adults and even gain media coverage, it is often the day-to-day traumatic experiences impacting so many children that are forgotten. Chronic experiences such as living at or below the poverty line aren't specific events but rather ongoing circumstances. An estimated 13.8 million children lived in poverty in the United States in 2017 (Child Poverty in America, 2017). Approximately 5.9 million of those children were under the age of six. Research has clearly demonstrated that living in poverty has a

1 OUT OF EVERY 4 CHILDREN ATTENDING SCHOOL HAS BEEN EXPOSED TO TRAUMATIC STRESS

14% OF CHILDREN HAVE EXPERIENCED ABUSE BY A CAREGIVER

OVER 1/3 OF STUDENTS HAVE BEEN BULLIED IN SCHOOL

wide range of negative effects on the physical and mental health of children. Poverty is a traumatic experience – it includes hunger, lack of adequate medical treatment, worry, and a multitude of other stressors.

> Trauma isn't always associated with violence. Divorce, a move, chronic worry, and health issues can all cause exaggerated and prolonged stress.

Traumatic events and toxic stress experiences negatively impact children and lead to changes in how they feel, behave, learn, view, and interact with others/themselves. How students perceive their stress and trauma is essential to understand as we implement the steps to creating a trauma-informed resilient school.

Schools represent an opportune system for prevention and early intervention across multiple domains related to positive childhood outcomes. As the prevalence and impact of trauma and traumatic stress become increasingly understood, the push for schools to become trauma-informed has also increased (SAMHSA, 2014). The National Center for Traumatic Stress Network (NCTSN) has issued a call to action for schools to play a key role in addressing the needs of traumatized children. Because such a large number of students are impacted by trauma, school professionals are

11% OF GIRLS AGES 14-17 HAVE EXPERIENCED SEXUAL ASSAULT

60% OF STUDENTS 17 YEARS OR YOUNGER HAVE BEEN EXPOSED TO CRIME, VIOLENCE, AND ABUSE

70% OF CHILDREN LIVING IN INNER CITY NEIGHBORHOODS ARE EXPOSED TO CHRONIC TOXIC STRESS

acutely aware of the challenges students face as a result of toxic stress and traumatic experiences. The creation of trauma-informed resilient schools must be a priority to support children's social, academic, and emotional development.

Since 1990, Starr Commonwealth has worked with thousands of professionals in both school and clinical settings who have taught us what matters most when working with stressed and traumatized children. This resource provides a comprehensive discussion, along with action steps to implement with individuals throughout the school system to most effectively answer NCTSN's call to action.

It is well documented that trauma can interfere with brain development, learning and behavior, and ability to develop relationships – all of which have a negative impact on a child's school success. By understanding the impact of trauma, educators can respond to youth in ways that reduce and even interrupt trauma's impact, support learning, and create positive school opportunities to foster and nurture resilience where students can thrive.

41% OF YOUTH UNDER 18 YEARS OLD REPORT EXPERIENCING A PHYSICAL ASSAULT IN THE LAST YEAR

25% OF CHILDREN IN THE UNITED STATES WITNESS/ EXPERIENCE A TRAUMATIC EVENT BEFORE THEY TURN 4 YEARS OLD

30% OF STUDENTS WHO ATTEND URBAN AREA SCHOOLS HAVE WITNESSED A STABBING OR A SHOOTING

Research indicates the following outcomes when schools are trauma-informed (Chafouleas et al, 2016):

Improved

- Academic achievement and test scores
- School climate
- Teacher sense of satisfaction and retention
- Graduation rates
- Community and family collaboration with school

Reduced

- Student behavioral outbursts and referrals
- Stress for staff and students
- Absences, detentions, and suspensions
- Student bullying, harassment, and fights
- Need for special education, services, and classes
- Drop-out rates

When school professionals see students through a "trauma-informed, resilience-focused lens" and recognize the impact of trauma – hidden risk factors, the role of fear in behaviors, and the unique physical needs and strengths of their students – they are able to approach students in ways that improve their ability to learn, connect with others, and develop resilience. At the heart of trauma-informed approaches in the school setting is the belief that student actions are the direct result of their experiences, and when students act out or disengage, the question we should ask is not, "what is wrong with you," but rather, "what has happened or what is happening to you?" By being informed about students' current and past experiences, educators can promote school engagement and success.

> "What is it about some students that allow them to thrive despite similar or even more significant exposure to trauma and toxic stress?"

The answer is found in characteristics of resilience and strengths. The term "resilience" is borrowed from the physics field and refers to the ability of an object or substance to "spring back" into shape (elasticity). When applied to people, resilience refers to one's ability to "bounce back" from adversity. Resilience characteristics have been reported to exist in children prior to trauma experiences (Bonanno, 2004). Children who demonstrate most of the psychological and emotional attributes associated with resilience, and whose social and family environment supports resiliency, may experience trauma symptoms after exposure to traumatic events. This is why we can't talk about trauma without talking about resilience, and why this book begins with a focus on resilience.

10 STEPS TO CREATE A TRAUMA-INFORMED RESILIENT SCHOOL

1   Focus on Resilience

2. Understand Trauma as an Experience

3. Foster Connections

4. Prioritize Social and Emotional Skill Development

5. Establish Safety

6. Promote Play and Breaks

7. Believe the Link Between Private Logic and Behavior

8. Partner with Families and Community

9. Support and Invest in Staff

10. Collect and Utilize Outcome Data

ABOUT THIS BOOK

The term educator is broadly used to refer to any school staff member who is involved in a child's educational experience, including principals, administrators, teachers, school psychologists, social workers, nurses, and paraprofessional staff.

This resource is divided into ten steps for educators to follow as they work towards the creation of trauma-informed resilient schools and classrooms. The steps start by focusing on resilience and then sharing a description of how trauma impacts children and their school experience. From there, each step provides detailed information and concrete actions that answer not just the "why" but also the "how" to create the best classroom and school supports for traumatized students and the school professionals who serve them.

The steps create a blueprint for trauma-informed resilient school implementation and success. It is impossible to select which one of the ten steps is most important. As you explore each of them, you will learn that parts of each step overlap. The steps are not linear or sequential, but instead they fit together like puzzle pieces. While creating a trauma-informed resilient school requires patience, with every small implementation you will see how each step complements another, and you will experience significant benefits in the overall school climate. You may even see that parts of a step, or even an entire step, may already be in place in your classroom or school.

 **How can I support a high school student whose mother has terminal cancer and is in hospice care? What is the right thing to say to him? How can I accommodate him?**

Your student is lucky to have a compassionate teacher who wants to say the right thing. You can let the student know you understand his mom is sick and you are available to talk. Ask if there is someone to support him at home. Sometimes all the focus shifts to the sick person, but others in the family suffer. Pay attention to changes in academics or behavior, and make accommodations if needed.

STEP 1

Focus on Resilience

We can't talk about making a school trauma-informed without talking about resilience.

> Resilience is the ability to achieve positive outcomes — mentally, emotionally, socially, and spiritually — despite adversity.

Resilience provides hope, which is essential for educators and their students. We may not be able to take away the toxic stress and trauma a child has experienced or will continue to encounter in their homes or communities, but we can create new experiences of resilience in our schools. The science of resilience tells us that every time a child has a positive interaction, we are not only protecting them to face future adversity but also helping them heal from the past. Being trauma-informed means we take all of a child's experiences into consideration. Being resilience-focused means we are always looking for new opportunities to provide students to uncover their hidden resilience and cultivate new characteristics of resilience to positively shift their view of self, others, and their environment.

As we begin to shift to a trauma-informed, resilience-focused mindset, it is helpful to introduce you to Starr Commonwealth and reflect on its core values and beliefs about children, which is deeply rooted in a resilience-focused mindset.

Starr Commonwealth dates back to 1913, when a young man named Floyd Starr purchased a barn and 40 scrub-covered acres in Albion, Michigan, to create refuge for "homeless, dependent, neglected, and delinquent boys." In his heart, he held a revolutionary belief that "there is no such thing as a bad child." With steadfast conviction and the support of his family, his "boys", and the commonwealth, he sought to help every child see and believe in their greatness.

Today, Starr Commonwealth continues to build on the legacy of "Uncle Floyd", and the tenet still holds true. Operating programs across globe, Starr offers community-based programs, residential treatment services, educational and behavioral health services, and professional training and coaching to heal trauma and build resilience in all children, adolescents, and the professionals that serve them.

Starr believes, as Uncle Floyd did, that when you treat a child with dignity and respect, it changes a child's heart. And that, in the end, is what changes a child's life. *10 Steps to Create a Trauma-Informed Resilient School* provides guidance to educators so you can be part of writing the many success stories that are waiting to be told. We are Driven to Heal. And together, we are building a bright future for all.

Floyd Starr wrote his creed in 1913. Over a century later, the core values and beliefs still constitute the trauma-informed, resilience-focused "treatment philosophy" of all Starr Commonwealth programs and services.

- We believe there is no such thing as a bad child.
- We believe that badness is not a normal condition but is the result of misdirected energy and unmet needs.
- We believe every child will be good if given an opportunity in an environment of love and activity.
- We believe in play. Play is a child's means of self-expression.
- We believe that children are resources.
- We believe that children merit confidence and trust.
- We believe that problems are opportunities.
- We believe that everyone has the responsibility to help and no one has the right to hurt.
- We believe beauty is a silent teacher.

It is a beneficial exercise to identify your own core values and beliefs about children. Our potential to shift towards a trauma-informed and resilience-focused mindset can be found within our core values and beliefs about children. Therefore, it may be a beneficial exercise to identify your own.

ACTIVITY:
Core Values and Beliefs

What are your core values and beliefs about children? What are the core values and beliefs about children in your school setting?

_____

_____

_____

_____

_____

RESILIENCE

If you scour resilience literature, you will find endless lists citing characteristics of resilient children. You will also find examples of experiences that will protect children when they face adversity. For example, psychological and emotional attributes and opportunities associated with resilience in children include: above average verbal skills, cognitive and problem solving opportunities and abilities, positive self-esteem, ability to self-regulate behavior, positive expectations about the future, familial and social supports (Loitre, Martin & Linares, 2005; Rice & Groves, 2005). However, there are four main factors that come up repeatedly, in almost every article, written about childhood resilience; 1) supportive adult-child relationships, 2) a sense of self-efficacy and perceived sense of control, 3) adaptive skills and self-regulatory capacities, 4) sources of faith, hope, and cultural traditions that provide meaning and a sense of value in life. It is interesting that these four main factors are the same factors identified by Starr Commonwealth's own Circle of Courage® model of resilience. This model has been used at Starr since 1989.

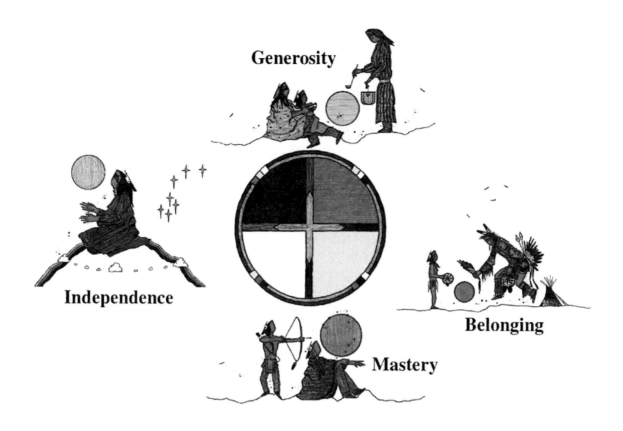

THE CIRCLE OF COURAGE®

The Circle of Courage® is a model of positive youth development based on the universal principle that to be emotionally healthy all youth need a sense of belonging, mastery, independence, and generosity. This unique model integrates the cultural wisdom of tribal peoples, the practice wisdom of professional pioneers with troubled youth, and findings of modern youth development research.

The four directions portray universal human needs for belonging, mastery, independence, and generosity. These are the foundations for psychological resilience and positive youth development.

Belonging

In Native American and First Nations cultures, significance was nurtured in communities of belonging. Lakota anthropologist Ella Deloria described the core value of belonging in these simple words: "Be related, somehow, to everyone you know." Treating others as kin forges powerful social bonds that draw all into relationships of respect. It was observed throughout history that the tribe, not the nuclear family, always ensured the survival of the culture.

Even if parents died or were not responsible, the tribe was always there to nourish the next generation. Adults and peers in the school setting are part of a child's tribe.

Mastery

Competence in traditional cultures is ensured by guaranteed opportunity for mastery. Children are taught to carefully observe and listen to those with more experience. A person with greater ability is seen as a model for learning, not as a rival. Each person strives for mastery for personal growth, but not to be superior to someone else. Humans have an innate drive to become competent and solve problems. With success in surmounting challenges, the desire to achieve is strengthened. The intent is to lead by example and be responsible. The school environment provides endless opportunities to experience mastery.

Independence

Power in Western culture is based on dominance, but in tribal traditions it means respecting the right for independence. In contrast to obedience models of discipline, Native teaching is designed to build respect and teach inner discipline. From earliest childhood, children are encouraged to make decisions, solve problems, and show personal responsibility. Adults model, nurture, teach values, and give feedback, but children are given abundant opportunities to make choices without coercion. In the school setting, this means that students can rely on adults and trust them at all times.

Generosity

Finally, virtue is reflected in the preeminent value of generosity. The central goal in Native American child-rearing is to teach the importance of being generous and unselfish. In the words of a Lakota Elder, "You should be able to give away your most cherished possession without your heart beating faster." In helping others, youth create their own proof of worthiness: they make a positive contribution to another human life, and in this self-value they find meaning for life.

Let's take a closer look at the four universal needs of the Circle of Courage®.

Belonging

I am important to someone and they want to know what my life is like – not only what I need help with but what my strengths are too.

The power and influence of positive human relationships in fostering resilience cannot be over-stated. Urie Bronfenbrenner, a developmental psychologist renowned for his ecological systems theory of child development, once stated that "every child needs at least one adult who is irrationally crazy about him or her." Bronfenbrenner believed this was the greatest factor contributing to one's healthy well-being later in life. Family and social environmental processes associated with resiliency include a stable, nurturing parent or caregiver, a connection to an adult in the extended family, and consistent family processes such as rituals, traditions, and structure. But when children have experienced or continue to experience trauma and toxic stress, sometimes the need for belonging is not met. What we know now is that if families can't always provide a sense of belonging and the connections children need, schools are the next best place to meet these needs. This is why the National Center for Traumatic Stress Network has issued a call to action for schools to play a critical role in addressing childhood trauma.

Trauma-informed, resilient schools and educators focus on what they can do, not on problems or deficits. Instead of saying, "This student is just going to go back to that situation on the weekend – what is the use?" they will say, "I am going to do whatever I can for this student while she is in my classroom or in my building to make her feel like she belongs here, is accepted, and cared about." When you are trauma-informed and resilience-focused, you seek solutions. Solutions are often found in opportunities to provide students with new experiences to have any one or more of their four universal needs met.

When the need for belonging is met, students are cooperative, make friends easily, and trust others. When feeling excluded, children experience pain and sadness and their self-esteem, self-regulation, and cognitive function decrease. Students who do not have their universal need of belonging met often withdraw, feel alienated, and lack trust. In an effort to have their belonging need met, they will often engage in behaviors like attention-seeking or clinging to teachers or peers.

Students lacking a sense of belonging often crave approval. Older students who are striving to have their need of belonging met sometimes engage is more extreme behaviors such as promiscuity or gang participation.

Responses from students of all ages when asked, "What is it like to belong at school?"
- Feeling safe when you are with the group.
- People at school know about the things that are important to you (family, pets, hobbies, etc.).
- Your ideas are important and valued by others.
- Being connected to the other people in school.
- You can make mistakes and not be judged by others.
- Teachers want to help you.
- Teachers care about you no matter what.
- Ability to rely on the other students.

School professionals can help students meet their need of belonging by being continuously curious about how the child is experiencing their world.
- Get to know them!
- Is there at least one adult at school the child can trust? If not, get them connected.
- Does the child feel like they belong at school?
- Do they have at least one or two close friends?
- Find out their likes and dislikes.
- Explore what students need most to feel supported and meet their potential.

Step 3 of this book will take you deeper into the importance of fostering connections in your school.

Mastery

For once, I feel like I am good at something – there is more to me than just the bad things that have happened in my life.

Mastery is the ability for someone to reach their potential with appropriate support(s) in place. When success is met, the desire to achieve and try new things is strengthened. Do not confuse mastery with perfection – everyone has an individualized level of mastery. When your need of mastery is being met, you believe you can rely on skills in a specific area, and use them to help navigate life and reach goals, cope with adversity, work through difficulties, and continue to strive to get better at something that is meaningful to you. In short, feeling a sense of mastery means you see yourself as capable and feel good about yourself. When a student's universal need of mastery is not met, they will appear as lazy and unmotivated. However, they are likely avoiding taking a risk for fear of failure. Students without strong mastery often give up easily and are failure- rather than success-oriented. Some students will engage in distorted behaviors in an attempt to get their need of mastery met. This includes cheating or engaging in delinquent skills (mastery in stealing without getting caught, selling drugs). These are likely coping skills learned by the child, and shouldn't be punished, but viewed as clues of the unmet need of mastery.

There are many areas in the school setting where students can experience mastery.
- Any subject: reading, vocabulary, comprehension, math facts, problem solving, science, social studies.
- Areas outside of the classroom: art, music, library, physical education, computer lab.
- Socially: making friends, keeping friends.
- Behaviorally: following school rules, making good choices.
- Understanding yourself and knowing what your body needs to stay regulated (nutrition, a break, a deep breath).
- Hobbies: sports, playing an instrument, being in a play.

Responses from students when asked, "How can educators help you meet your universal need of mastery?"
- Celebrate your accomplishments and hard work.

- Answer questions, give tips, explain something differently if we don't understand it the first way it is explained.
- Encourage and motivate you.
- Notice when things are difficult and support you.
- Plan cooperative activities in class, not ones that make me compete with others.

School professionals can help students meet their need of mastery by identifying each student's potential and providing the necessary supports to get them there.

- Teach emotional awareness and regulation.
- Provide opportunities for students to use their strengths.
- Set short and long term goals, and offer praise as student makes progress.
- Encourage students to persist even when a task is challenging.
- Embrace the motto: "Progress over perfection".
- Have students solve problems out loud. This slows down the process of critical thinking and analysis.
- Pose open-ended questions about assignments or skills.
- Tell me what you know about…
- Ask student, how you break this problem down into smaller steps… (i.e., how can you first get from _____ to _____?)

Independence
I have a choice. I can help make decisions.
I can solve problems when I am supported by an adult.

Students need independence that is guided and supported by a caring adult. Students feel a sense of independence when they have choice. Independence helps to increase motivation and engagement, and helps to meet individual learner needs, allowing students to capitalize on strengths. Students feel autonomy not only when they understand a task or a rule but see the value of that task or rule. When students have their need of independence met, they have self-control, are assertive, are responsible, and are usually leaders in your classroom or school. When the need of independence is absent, students will lack confidence, control, and will be easily mislead. You may describe them as irresponsible or hopeless. Distorted ways of getting the need of independence may appear rebellious, overly controlled, manipulative, reckless, and as bullies. When a student does not have a healthy level of independence it is likely because they were not taught the skills they need to be independent, or because they were forced to be independent too early. If this is the case, they need to be taught and they will need to practice independence skills.

When students are asked what independence means to them, these are their responses:

- Make safe and healthy choices.
- Solve problems.
- Know your feelings and help yourself get calm when upset.
- Think for yourself (it is OK if you have different ideas than other people).
- Make good choices for yourself (cleaning up after yourself, putting things away, doing homework or chores without being reminded).
- Not always doing what you want, just because you want, but consider others and what they might want or need.

When students are asked how educators can help them meet their universal need of independence, these are their responses:

- Help you do things by yourself after giving you support.
- Support you when you try new things.
- Remind you of things you can do when upset.
- Help you to solve tough problems.

Additional ideas for school professionals to help students meet their need of independence:

- Invite students to help decide classroom rules.
- Post and review classroom rules regularly.
- Teach students how to use planners to keep track of assignments and to set goals.
- Provide choices.
- Provide options for the best ways students can be ready to learn.
- Use calming corners or other in-classroom ways to cope with stress and frustration.

Generosity
In helping others, we create our own proof of worthiness and self-value.

When students have the opportunity to help others, they feel valuable. So many times, children who have experienced a lifetime of toxic stress or trauma do not believe they have anything to offer another person. Instead, they have been on the receiving end of "help". When a child experiences helping another person, they feel a sense of meaning, purpose, and even pride. Students who have their need of generosity met will be caring, compassionate, empathetic, and unselfish. Students who do not have their need met often appear hopeless, cold, hardened, and unworthy.

Responses from students when asked, "What does generosity mean to you?"
- Helping someone when they are having a hard time.
- Participating in a community event – volunteering, participating in a fundraiser, etc.
- Saving money and buying something for parent.
- Spending time making a gift for a friend or teacher.
- Helping in the classroom by putting things away, helping the teacher with jobs.
- Teaching something I know to someone who needs help learning.

When students are asked how educators can help them meet their need of generosity, these are their responses:
- Take time to notice when students are generous.
- Give students compliments.
- Give students opportunities to help in the classroom.
- Provide time for partner work and group work.
- Help students understand how other people are feeling.

Other ideas for school professionals to help students meet their need of generosity:
- Age-appropriate tasks to help peers, teachers, other adult professionals in the school setting.
- Use classroom meeting time to provide compliments to others (remember to focus on actions rather than physical compliments about looks, clothing, etc.).

- Remind students about ways to be kind and helpful to others.
- Participate in a school activity or community service project.
- Ask students to notice when other students are being generous.
- Always model kindness and respect (never make a student earn it).

The developmental needs of children are universal. In training over 60,000 professionals who work with children around the globe in a variety of settings and cultural contexts, not one person, group, or community has said, "No, we do not see belonging, mastery, independence, and/or generosity as important." In fact, we have found that these four areas are universally accepted and valued. Of course, not all resilient children possess all of these attributes, nor do all of these characteristics exist to the same degree in children. It is therefore reasonable to hypothesize that factors of resilience exist in several combinations, and psychological and emotional traits exists to a greater or lesser extent in children. Family and social environmental supports range from many to modest. We can then assume that a child with several psychological, emotional, family, and social characteristics associated with resilience may be the most resilient, and children with fewer may be less resilient. Consequently, exposure to toxic stress and trauma may result in fairly rapid returns to pre-trauma functioning for children at the high end of the continuum of resilience and more prolonged struggle with trauma related symptoms and reactions for less resilient children. Being trauma-informed means that we need to look for hallmarks of resilience students possess, and it means that we must help children build characteristics of resilience and draw upon their strengths through the interactions and opportunities we provide to them in the classroom and school setting (Steele, Raider & Kuban, 2007).

So let's return to the four main protective factors we see in the resilience literature today.
- Supportive adult-child relationships.
- A sense of self-efficacy and perceived sense of control.
- Adaptive skills and self-regulatory capacities.
- Sources of faith, hope, and cultural traditions that provide meaning and a sense of value.

Supportive adult-child relationships meet the universal need of belonging. A sense of mastery is met when a child has a sense of self-efficacy and perceived control. Independence is achieved when children have adaptive skills and self-regulatory capacities. Feeling a sense of self-value and ability to have something to offer others meets the universal need of generosity. The same core values and beliefs applied through the Circle of Courage® resilience model are the same key factors protecting children from adversity and improving their resilience today. When we focus on resilience, we find hope, solutions, and even joy. We also begin to bring out the best in ourselves, as well as our students. This is what can help keep us motivated despite the adversity we see our student's experience. We matter, and the experiences we provide our students matter. We can provide opportunities every day for the students in our classrooms and buildings to have their needs of belonging, mastery, independence, and generosity met.

You will learn more about assessing the universal needs of children and ways to implement the principles of the Circle of Courage® again in this book in Step 7.

The Circle of Courage® Tier 1 Supports Self Reflection on the following pages is a tool for educators. This resource helps educators identify several examples of tier 1 support strategies for each universal need that makes up the Circle of Courage®. Educators are encouraged to rate the frequency of the implementation of the strategies every one or two months over the course of the school year. There is not a scoring key for this tool. It is designed to help educators self-reflect and assess how often they are utilizing proactive strategies with students.

Tier I Circle of Courage® Staff Self-Assessment: Belonging

Name: _____   Date: _____

Directions: Please rate your implementation of the following four universal need interventions; Belonging, Mastery, Independence, and Generosity based upon the following scale: 0 - Not yet implemented, 1 - Rarely implemented, 2 - Sometimes, 3 - Almost always, 4 - Always. After you rate the interventions, take a look at the numbers you selected for each intervention. Focus on one to two interventions from each universal need category where you rated yourself with a 0, 1, or 2 for the next several weeks. Feel proud of the interventions you are consistently implementing almost always and/or all of the time. Well done! Periodically, come back to this assessment to compare how you are doing with your implementation.

Rate your implementation of the following interventions to support BELONGING:

	0 Not Yet Implemented	1 Rarely Implemented	2 Sometimes	3 Almost Always	4 Always
1. I greet each student by name every day and when they want to be called, if they have a nickname and how to pronounce it.					
2. I have asked each student what they want to be called, if they have a nickname and how to pronounce it.					
3. I strive to establish a positive relationship with every student (trust, connection, and understanding) and assume each student is doing their best. Example: You look tired today – is that why you haven't started your work? and, Do you need a drink of water, a few minutes, some time to help you get started? (Give time to let them respond).					
4. I have daily classroom meetings.					
5. I have created norms for classroom meetings collectively with my students.					
6. I practice pro-social behaviors during classroom meetings with my students.					
7. I implement the 5:1 positive/negative interactions rule. (I always look for the good in every situation. I notice what is going right. Have at least 5 positive interactions for every 1 negative interaction.)					
8. I offer specific verbal affirmation for students who are making another student(s) feel a sense of belonging.					
9. When a difficult behavior arises, I do my best to look beyond the behavior to determine if the behavior is a bid for connection.					
10. I respond to student's bids for connection within boundaries.					
11. I restore relationships after negative interactions between myself and a student and/or between students. (Mediation session with teacher and student and/or peer to peer—may need to wait until all parties are calm.)					
12. I use time-in strategies.					
13. If a student has to leave the classroom to regain regulation, I wholeheartedly welcome them back.					
14. I notice strengths in every student.					
15. I provide opportunities for students to work together in structured and unstructured groups each day.					
16. I role model valuing diversity and acceptance and infuse this into curriculum (i.e. through "read alouds", science, history, math role models, etc.).					
17. I identify students' interests and hobbies and find something you have in common with every student.					
18. I help students see what they have in common with each other.					

© Starr Commonwealth 2019

Page 1 of 5

STARR COMMONWEALTH

Rate your implementation of the following interventions to support BELONGING continued:	0 Not Yet Implemented	1 Rarely Implemented	2 Sometimes	3 Almost Always	4 Always
19. I teach and role play social skills and problem solving (SEL curriculum, classroom meetings, integrate into subject areas: act out characters, perform skits and plays, job skills/math, role models in history, etc.).					
20. When a student is struggling to connect, I use the 2:10 strategy – 2 minute conversation for 10 days consecutively about something not academically related to build relationship.					
21. I check in with students frequently, giving feedback every hour.					
22. I laugh and play with students every day.					
23. I celebrate reaching goals collectively.					
24. I speak regularly about what belonging means to my and the students in my classroom.					
25. I display anchor charts in my classroom that promote belonging.					
26. I promote positive speech about students and their families with colleagues.					
27. I use gender neutral pronouns – (i.e. they, them, everyone).					
Self-Reflection:					
Date #1:					
Date #2:					
Date #3:					
Date #4:					

Rate your implementation of the following interventions to support MASTERY:

	0 Not Yet Implemented	1 Rarely Implemented	2 Sometimes	3 Almost Always	4 Always
1. I post and review classroom rules regularly.					
2. I self-reflect and ask myself, "What am I teaching and reinforcing?"					
3. I self-reflect and ask myself, "How am I treating my students, peers and parents – am I modeling the behavior I want to see in my students?" (Perseverance, calm, patience, generosity, empathy)					
4. I ask myself, "Do all students understand the rules and have the capability/social skills to carry them out?"					
5. When giving instructions I provide clearly stated and specifically identified expectations.					
6. I repeat expectations frequently.					
7. I consistently offer students opportunities for process based praise.					
8. I consistently offer students opportunities for peer-to-peer feedback.					
9. I use flexible student groupings to teach and reteach as needed.					
10. I use students as resources.					
11. I celebrate accomplishments and goals collectively.					
12. I get to know all of my students' strengths and interests.					
13. I make sure everyone knows each other's strengths and expertise.					
14. I check in with all students frequently and offer individualized and specific feedback for each child.					
15. I promote a growth mindset by focusing on how much students have learned and remind them of the power of the word, "yet" (i.e. maybe you aren't there yet, but you are making such great progress).					
16. As an educator, I am always in the process of learning.					
17. I provide myself with opportunities for self-care on a daily basis.					

Self-Reflection:

Date #1:

Date #2:

Date #3:

Date #4:

Rate your implementation of the following interventions to support INDEPENDENCE:	0 Not Yet Implemented	1 Rarely Implemented	2 Sometimes	3 Almost Always	4 Always
1. I frequently pause and check in with my own level of emotional regulation.					
2. I teach and practice mind body skills for emotional awareness and regulation every day to promote relaxation and access to coping skills. Skills such as: breathing and movement exercises, body scans, guided imagery, and mindfulness.					
3. During classroom meetings I practice noticing and naming feelings with my students.					
4. I provide students access to sensory tools such as fidgets, weighted lap pads, exercise balls.					
5. I provide students with an opportunity to lead one another in emotional awareness and regulation practices.					
6. I give students choices of how to cope when they are having a hard day.					
7. I offer frequent opportunities for movement throughout each day.					
8. I seek out additional proactive breaks for students who have more sensory needs.					
9. I attune myself to a student's body language in order to get a sense of where they are in terms of emotional regulation.					
10. I use affective statements and questions.					
11. I post and review classroom expectations daily.					
12. I provide students with a daily planner or goal sheet.					
13. I provide a written class agenda on the board daily.					
14. I give choices whenever possible.					
15. I include students in on decision making.					
16. I include students in on problem solving.					
17. I encourage students to take appropriate challenges.					
18. I ensure students you are there to help and support them.					
19. I teach students about the impact of stress and trauma on the brain (i.e. use the meerkat, tiger, and owl example).					
20. I implement movement in the classroom every day.					
21. I provide alternate seating.					
22. I provide an open option for a "calm down" spot or corner in my classroom.					
Self-Reflection:					
Date #1:					
Date #2:					
Date #3:					
Date #4:					

© Starr Commonwealth 2019

Rate your implementation of the following interventions to support GENEROSITY:

	0 Not Yet Implemented	1 Rarely Implemented	2 Sometimes	3 Almost Always	4 Always
1. I speak regularly with my class about what generosity means to all of us.					
2. I display anchor charts in my classroom that support generosity.					
3. I offer specific verbal affirmation when other students are showing generosity towards another student.					
4. I offer classroom jobs to all students.					
5. I practice solving problems during classroom meetings.					
6. I practice giving compliments during classroom meetings.					
7. I create opportunities for students to help each other and showcase their strengths.					
8. I have students write notes or make cards to show appreciation to their families, school, and greater community.					
9. I promote service learning projects. Let students' passions be the driver (e.g. love of animals – bottle drive and donate proceeds to animal shelter).					
10. I teach and practice empathy exercises for self and others.					
11. I model kindness and generosity.					
12. When a student is struggling with a behavior, I offer them a suggestion to redirect their energy in a helpful way. For example, a student is struggling to stay in their seat, invite them to carry library books down to the library.					

Self-Reflection:

Date #1:

Date #2:

Date #3:

Date #4:

ACTIVITY:
Strengths Inventory

Every child has strengths. It should be common practice to conduct a strengths inventory on every student in your school. While there are several inventories on the market that help assess strengths, you may also choose to do your own inventory on your own or with colleagues. Here is a simple strengths inventory that is not only easy to use, but extremely informative. Information provided from a strengths inventory can help with student regulation, inform behavior plans, and drive intervention strategies.

See below for an example of how to fill out the Strengths Inventory Activity. You can use the words listed on the activity sheet or use your own.

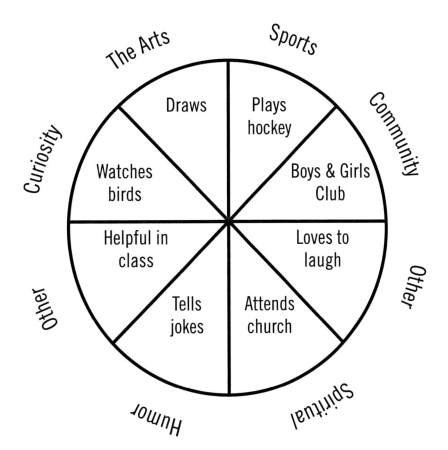

_____ # Strengths Inventory
Name

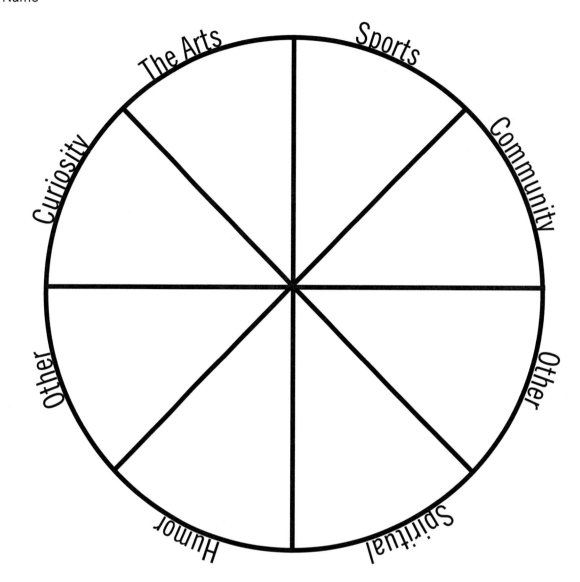

EXAMPLE OF WORDS TO USE WHEN COMPLETING THE INVENTORY:

Creativity	Honesty	Generous
Curiosity	Love	Patient
Critical thinking	Kindness	Self-regulated
Likes to learn	Social skills	Gratitude
Wisdom	Teamwork	Hope
Courage	Leadership	Humor
Perseverance	Ability to forgive	

Children of trauma need to feel they're good at something. Find opportunities to allow kids to set and achieve goals, and they'll feel a sense of mastery. Assign jobs in the classroom that they can do well, or encourage them to be a peer helper to someone else. Set them up to succeed, and provide them with experiences that allow them to feel their worth through concrete tasks.

Remember this...

STEP 1 HIGHLIGHTS
Resilience-building experiences

- We may not be able to change a student's experiences of stress and trauma, but we can provide them with new resilience experiences.
- There is no such thing as a bad child.
- The four universal needs of all people are belonging, mastery, independence, and generosity.
- Regularly reflect on your implementation of activities and strategies to support the four universal needs in your classroom/school.

STEP 2

Understanding Trauma as an Experience

Every person who works in a school setting should have awareness and knowledge about childhood trauma, its signs and symptoms, and the impact it has on learning and behavior. Trauma-informed professionals view others from a place of curiosity and are always wondering "What has happened or what is currently happening in a person's life that is impacting how they think, behave, and interact with others?" Instead of focusing on behavior as a problem or possible diagnosis, understanding trauma and toxic stress encourage the exploration of what might be driving behavior, providing a better understanding of what that person needs most. In the school setting, trauma-informed professionals do not only view students in this way, but approach all staff, parents, and volunteers with curiosity.

CASE EXAMPLE: ED

A third grade teacher was teaching a lesson on conjugating verbs into the past tense. Each student was expected to come to the front of the class and make the necessary changes to their assigned word. One student, seated in the back of the classroom, was assigned a word that needed "-ed" added to the end of it in order for it to be conjugated properly. When it was his turn to approach the board and write these two letters next to the word, he froze and refused to come forward. After some coaxing from his teacher and stares from the rest of the class, he walked to the board and picked up a marker. Just as he was about to write, he started yelling, crying, and flipped over a nearby table. The teacher immediately removed the rest of the students from the classroom, and an administrator came down to the room to calm the student down.

What would be learned later is that the name of the man molesting the young boy was Ed.

Educators who witness reactions like this often jump to attaching labels to the behavior, and ultimately the student: aggressive, violent, emotionally-disturbed, oppositional, and defiant. To them, the behavior does not make sense and is irrational. Therefore, it must be controlled, extinguished, medicated, or punished. As one can see in the "Ed" example, the behavior made more sense than anyone expected. In that student's brain, an alarm was sounding; "ed" meant danger.

The first warning sign of this was his "frozen" state in the back of the room. Once pressured to come forward, his brain selected a "fight" response. Obviously, this teacher had no way of knowing in the moment why her student was reacting the way he was, but trauma sensitivity doesn't require that we know who is traumatized, or in what way they were traumatized. Instead, it is how we react to behavior that matters most. Thankfully, in this case, someone asked the right questions to find out the truth. How often does that fail to happen? How often do we label and punish these kids, focusing on what's wrong with them rather than what they are experiencing and what has happened to them?

"People think I am just a mean person, but I'm really not - I have to act that way or else they will try to hurt me and I can't let that happen — I have been hurt too many times before." –Megan

Contrary to what many school professionals think, you do not have to be a school social worker, counselor, or psychologist to provide trauma-informed care and practice. Any person, regardless of their own background and role in the school setting, can be trauma-informed and help students thrive academically, behaviorally, socially, and emotionally when they understand how stress and trauma impact students. Many educators have concerns about becoming trauma-informed. Some fear any involvement with their students' traumatic and stressful experiences. Others feel overwhelmed with the demands of curriculum and behavior management, and worry about adding another responsibility to their workloads. Others, upon hearing the word "trauma," immediately imagine something far too painful to witness. These responses are common and they are normal. Trauma is terrorizing, not just for the victims, but also for those who witness events and hear about the experiences. These feelings must be acknowledged and then followed with a discussion about what being trauma-informed really means.

> "My migraines started right after my parents were arrested and I went into foster care. My head always hurts, that is normal — but sometimes it hurts so bad I can't stand up to get ready for school." –Jada

It may come as a pleasant surprise for school professionals that being trauma-informed and providing trauma-informed care doesn't require knowing the details of a child's traumatic experience(s). Trauma-informed care doesn't dictate that traumatic experiences must be discussed or processed. Instead, being trauma-informed means that professionals learn how to view all students through a curious lens that helps them explore how students view themselves, others, and the world around them as a result of their unique experiences. With this knowledge, school professionals can create a school climate that provides traumatized children with what they need most to best develop and thrive. Providing students with opportunities to experience safety, consistency, understanding, connections, and support are key components of trauma-informed care. Every person in every position who makes a decision that impacts students, or who works directly or indirectly with children in a school system, needs to learn about childhood trauma.

A generic school district organizational chart is located on the next page. As you implement the steps in this book, find your own school or district organizational chart and identify each person, group, or department who will need to receive training about trauma-informed resilient school implementation.

> You don't need to know exactly what caused or is causing the trauma to help. Instead of focusing on the specifics of a traumatic experience, educators can support children by concentrating on a student's worry, hurt, or anger. You don't have to dig deep to be able to effectively respond with flexibility and empathy.

UNDERSTANDING TRAUMA

ACUTE TRAUMA

A single-time, limited event. e.g., witness an accident, medical or dental procedure, death, move.

CHRONIC TRAUMA

Multiple traumatic exposures and/or events over extended periods of time e.g., bullying, domestic violence.

ACUTE STRESS

Normal response to stress and trauma that lasts for 4-6 weeks.

TOXIC STRESS

Adverse experiences that lead to strong, frequent, or prolonged activation of the body's stress response system in the absence of the buffering protection of a supportive adult relationship* e.g., neglect, abuse, poverty, homelessness, community violence, war.

POST-TRAUMATIC STRESS
(CHRONIC TRAUMA AND TOXIC STRESS)

This is also a normal response to stress and trauma, but because it is prolonged and exaggerated and lasts much longer than acute stress, the result is significant dysregulation of a person's central nervous system.

Trauma activates the body's stress response system. When this happens heart rate, respiration, muscle tension, and blood flow increase because of the body's cortisol and adrenalin surge.

When this activation, which is only meant to be short term, is prolonged, there is a compromise to the functions of the brain.

*Shonkoff et al, 2012

Who Needs to Receive Childhood Trauma Training?

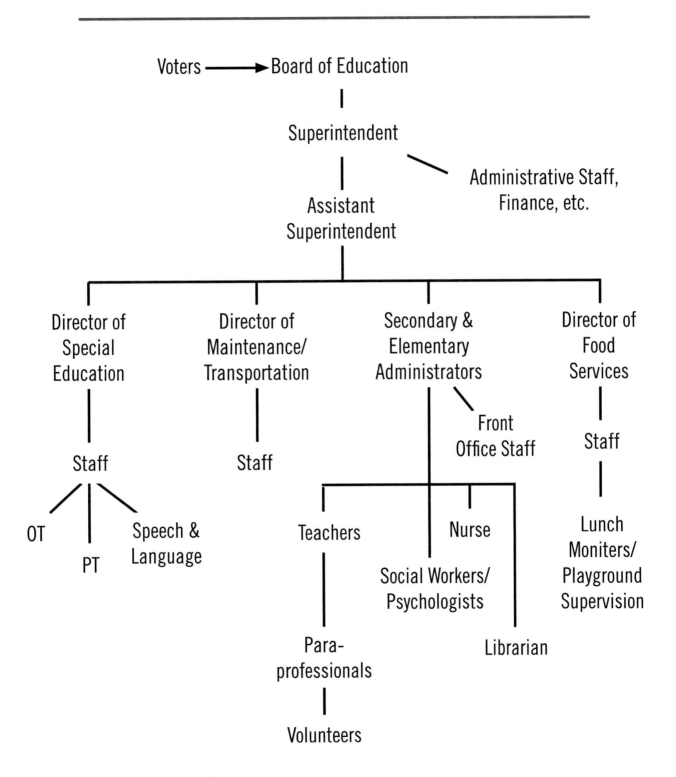

Exposure & Experiences

Children and adolescents are in a constant state of development, and their life experiences can influence their physical and emotional growth in both positive and negative ways. Physiological changes to developing brains, and their emotional and behavioral responses to trauma, have the potential to significantly interfere with their school life. While brain development occurs mostly during the first years of life, and then again during adolescence, the brain develops well into early adulthood (Anderson & Teicher, 2008). This means that early traumatic experiences, as well as those happening during adolescence, can profoundly impact and limit brain development in negative ways. The impact can result in the loss of cognitive function; physical and emotional dysregulation and social delays; and problems with memory and problem solving, all of which undermine learning and compromise a child's school experience.

SPECTRUM OF TRAUMA

Traumatic experiences change the structure and functioning of a child's brain when the activation of the stress response system is long lasting. When exposed to a stressor, everyone's body responds through either one or more fight, flight, or freeze responses. When this happens, activated systems throughout the body release stress hormones that are designed to be protective for survival. However, these responses are supposed to last only a short time. When exaggerated and prolonged, rather than protective responses, they become dangerous to the brain and lead to negative implications for brain development, regulation, and social functioning.

The American Academy of Pediatrics (AAP) warns that extended exposure to toxic stress can lead to functional changes in several regions of the brain involved in learning and behavior, including the amygdala, hippocampus, and prefrontal cortex (Shonkoff et al, 2012). Neuroimaging techniques show that some brain regions actually reduce in size as a result of childhood maltreatment. Others become enlarged and hypersensitive. This clearly indicates the brain structure and chemistry are affected for students who are stressed, anxious, or insecure. A study conducted with at-risk children during the summer months, and then again during the early weeks of school, showed a dramatic 53% increase when school started in the stress chemical adrenalin, which activates our bodies. In addition, there was a 13% decrease at the start of the school year compared with the summer months in brain chemicals that have a calming effect. These shifts were associated with an increase in anxiety, withdrawal, thinking, and learning problems during the initial weeks of school. This type of stress reactivity is all too common in children with histories of trauma, and exposure to chronic stress and results in academic, behavioral, and relational challenges (Call, Purvis, Parris & Cross, 2014).

"I cried in the drop-off line at school every day. My mom didn't know why and when she asked me, I just couldn't speak. That made her mad. But my words wouldn't even come out if I wanted them to. Then one night I felt brave when she was tucking me in to go to bed and then I told her what the girls at school say to me — about my weight and about her [Mom's] weight. They tease me and my Mom — they call us pigs, fat pigs. I just can't face them." *—Jai'lyn*

Changes in the brain are the reason why there is a significant correlation between trauma and low academic achievement. Children who have experienced trauma often find it more difficult than their peers to pay attention, as well as process and recall new information heard during classroom instruction. In a sample of high-risk children who were exposed to more than four negative childhood experiences, all were more likely to have learning and behavior problems than their peers without adverse experiences. Other studies show children exposed to violence score lower on IQ and reading ability tests than their peers. Maltreated children are more likely than their peers to be retained in a grade, miss school, and be placed in special education. Children with more exposure to violence also have lower grade point averages than children with less exposure to violence (Center on the Developing Child at Harvard University, 2007).

Stress and trauma impact learning because of the effects on the functions of the brain. Let's take a closer look at the primary functions of the brain impacted by trauma.

FUNCTIONS OF THE BRAIN

BRAIN STEM FUNCTIONS

The brain stem is responsible for body functions that are involuntary and automatic, such as the regulation of breathing, heart rate, and body temperature. The important thing to remember about the brain stem is that it works without us thinking about it. When we are exposed to intense stress or trauma, the brain stem is activated. This is the part of the brain that is responsible for the fight, flight, and freeze survival responses that happen during stress and trauma.

Imagine what happens in your own body during intense fear or stress. Think about how your body responds. Does your heart start to beat faster? Does your breathing become more rapid or shallow? Do you get hot or sweaty? Do your muscles become tense? The answer to each question is "yes". These reactions happen because your brain stem becomes activated when you are faced with something that requires your attention and survival. All of the responses are automatic and occur without thought or intention.

"When I am alone, I panic. I want to jump out of my skin. I just want someone there, or I need to just knock myself out —either with weed or a sleeping pill."

–Kathleen

The brain stem is the deepest part of the brain, and sits at the top of our spinal cord. Keep in mind that the brain stem is intimately connected with the sensory part of our brain. You will see how the brain stem activates certain responses in our bodies depending upon our sensory experiences. Let's discuss that now.

> "I get so nervous and then I start tripping,
> or bumping into things, or breaking things,
> spilling things – one leads to the next – it is
> so embarrassing but I just can't control it. My
> body gets so clumsy and I just feel crazy."
> –*John*

SENSORY BRAIN FUNCTIONS

This part of the brain is responsible for many things, but the main functions to highlight here are related to sensation, self-regulation, and memory. As mentioned, the parts of the brain responsible for these functions are located in close proximity to the brain stem. The brain stem plays a key role with sensory brain functions and regulation of emotions and behavior. When exposed to stress, trauma, or body memories prompted by our senses, our brain stem will either activate or remain calm. For example, when we smell or taste sour milk, our body responds. When we touch a hot pan, our body responds. When we hear a loud noise, our body responds. Almost immediately, we respond to sensory inputs, especially those that make us suspicious about our safety or the safety of others. If something doesn't look, smell, taste, or feel right, we experience a body response alerting us to the potential harm. These body responses are mitigated by the functions of our deep, sensory brain. Overall, these negative experiences or memories of them make us dysregulated (our brain stem will make our heart beat faster and our breathing shallower). In comparison, when we smell something soothing like lavender, or smell something such as homemade cookies that reminds us of a good time in our life, we feel calm and content because our brain stem is not triggered to activate or engage in a survival response.

SENSES

Identification of sensations is one of the main functions of the deep, sensory part of the brain. At birth, the brain functions responsible for sensation are working. While our senses become more refined as we develop, it is interesting to know and remember that they are all functioning immediately at birth, and are responsible for how we experience ourselves, others, and the environment around us.

An infant can see. Visual acuity improves as the infant develops, but an infant can see contrasting patterns and shapes, especially the facial features of a caregiver. An infant can hear. We know that infants startle when they hear loud noises and calm to the sound of a caregiver's voice. An infant can taste. This is why infant formula is created to resemble the taste of sweet, fatty breast milk. An infant can smell. In fact, there have been studies that show infants can pick out the scent of their mother from several other mothers. Infants can feel senses of touch. We know what happens when their diapers are wet or when they receive one of their first immunizations – they cry! Disruption of any one of an infant's sensations creates stress and activates their brain stem. As a result, an infant's heart rate, respiration, and muscle tension will increase. This is visible when an infant is crying, or when a toddler is having a tantrum. Sensations are disrupted, there is stress, the brain stem is activated, and we see dysregulation.

While these examples are related to infants, keep in mind everyone becomes dysregulated to some extent when their senses are disrupted. Imagine what happens in your body when you hear a loud noise, smell smoke, taste spoiled milk, or feel a needle on your skin. You startle, pupils dilate – your body reacts, your brain stem is activated, it causes some degree of stress and without even thinking about it, and you respond. You become acutely attuned to the sensations and you will often try to get away from the situation (flight), fight it off, or stay very still (freeze) in the first moments after you experience the sensation.

> "I need to move, my legs, they get busy – I have to run. I can't stay in the class for a minute longer." –James

SELF-REGULATION

When one of our senses is activated, we have either a pleasant or an unpleasant experience. For example, if an infant can't see their primary caregiver, if their diaper is wet, or if they are hungry, they become dysregulated. If they are fed, warm, and dry, then they are likely to be content. Imagine for a minute how a parent or caregiver responds when they are with an infant who is crying. Likely, through another sensory input like holding, rocking, or singing softly, we try to calm down the reaction of the stress system (activated by the brain stem) that exposure to that sensation has caused. This is accomplished by engaging in an activity that helps reduce the over-activation of the brain stem. Rocking actually helps to rest the heart rate to the optimal 60-80 beats per minute, and is why it is such a successful activity for children who are upset, and for adults who enjoy rocking on their porch swing for relaxation.

MEMORY

When an infant is picked up, rocked, comforted, changed, fed, or burped in response to their dysregulation, they likely calm down. We respond to their dysregulation by trying to reconcile the disruption of their senses. When an infant's needs are met in this way over and over again during the first weeks and months of their life, memories are created. Memories of trust, consistency, and an implicit knowing that, "When I signal discomfort, someone is going to help me feel better" are formed. Now, imagine for a minute an infant who is crying and dysregulated. This time, there is not a parent or caregiver who responds consistently to their needs. For example, the parent or caregiver has mental health challenges, abuses drugs, or neglects the infant. In this case, the infant isn't re-regulated with the help of a caregiving relationship, or maybe sometimes they are attended to and sometimes they aren't. In this case, the infant doesn't create a memory that is rooted in trust. Instead, the memories created are those of distrust, inconsistency, and fear.

SENSES <—> AFFECT/STRESS REGULATION <—> MEMORY

In a perfect world, there is balance and integration between the main brain functions driving our sensations, stress-regulation, and memory. However, when there is stress or trauma – especially when prolonged – these brain functions become dysregulated. As a result, they don't work well

together because there is disruption of sensations, dysregulation, and no memories to draw upon to signal to that person how to help themselves regain a balanced state.

In trauma, the functions of the sensory brain are working overtime.

Symptoms of trauma resulting from the stress impact on the sensory brain:

- Sensory input disruption and overwhelming (sights, sounds, smells).
- Dysregulated central nervous system.
- Difficulty managing emotions and behavior.
- Hyperactive, jumpy, nervous.

In the classroom, when the sensory brain is working overtime, educators see:

- Students easily triggered by what they hear, see, or smell.
- Reactive students.
- Students who can't sit still, stay seated, or listen.

THINKING BRAIN FUNCTIONS

This part of the brain is responsible for many things, but its main functions are language, learning, cognition, problem solving, decision making, and impulse control.

> "Sometimes, when my younger sister screams, it reminds me of everyone screaming on the beach when my friend drowned two years ago. It's like it's happening all over again. I even feel the panic in my stomach." —Jamal

---

LANGUAGE

The Broca's area of the brain is the part of the brain responsible for language. This part of the brain is compromised during stress and trauma. An example of this is when a person is upset or angry and they can't find the words to speak. Or, when they remember something that happened but they can't find the words to describe what they experienced. This is why children of trauma not only don't want to talk about things that happened, but actually can't – this is why when we ask, "What happened or why did you do that?" we hear responses like "I don't know." Often, there aren't even words — only shrugged shoulders or a blank stare.

LEARNING & COGNITION

The hippocampus, the part of the brain involved in learning and cognition, is compromised by the stress response. The hippocampus becomes damaged when stress and trauma experiences are prolonged, and the damage actually leads to a decrease in the hippocampal volume of this structure. Not only does this compromise a student's ability to remember what was learned in the past, it makes it difficult for students to learn new information (Saigh & Bremner, 1999).

PROBLEM SOLVING, DECISION MAKING, & IMPULSE CONTROL

The prefrontal cortex helps us to plan and control impulses, become mentally attuned to others, empathize with them, and provides us with a moral awareness. It also provides us with insight and logic allowing us to problem solve and make decisions. Like the hippocampus, the prefrontal cortex is impacted by stress, and may not physically develop to its usual size or be of a smaller volume than average following trauma experiences that are exaggerated or prolonged.

> In trauma, the functions of the thinking brain DO NOT work well. In other words, stressed brains can't learn.

Symptoms of trauma resulting from the stress impact on the thinking brain:
- Difficulty concentrating.
- Problem solving is a challenge.
- Can't find the words to describe what you know.

In the classroom, when the thinking brain is compromised educators see:
- Difficulties with processing verbal information.
- Problems focusing.
- Problems following teacher directions.
- Difficulty recalling what was heard and retaining information.

Additionally, these cognitive deficits often result in:
- Low self-esteem.
- Poor problem solving.
- Increased truancy.
- Behavior issues.
- Hopelessness.
- Increased peer conflict.
- Increased dropout rates.

Trauma-informed resilient schools understand the impact stress and trauma have on children and their ability to regulate emotions, behavior, and ultimately learning. We can't ignore the impact trauma has on students if our education systems are going to meet the demands of parents, communities, and funders.

> There is a direct connection between stress and learning. When kids are stressed, it's tough for them to learn. Create a safe, accepting environment in your classroom by empathizing with students situations and showing support. The more educators can do to reduce anxiety in the classroom, the more likely for increased academic performance.

UNDERSTAND TRAUMA'S IMPACT

Use the activity on page 39 with staff, parents, or students to teach them how trauma impacts the brain.

SCREENING STUDENTS FOR TOXIC STRESS AND TRAUMA

According a survey by The National Child and Traumatic Stress Network, few schools have protocols in place to obtain trauma histories for students. This becomes especially problematic for students who transfer from another school or district. Children often transfer schools because of potentially traumatizing or stressful events such as a change in living situation. By creating a standardized protocol to assess exposure to potentially traumatizing incidents in the past or present among students, the school can immediately understand how they can best meet a student's unique behavior and learning needs. Starr recommends completing a Life Events Checklist available at starr.org/store.

SIGNS AND SYMPTOMS THAT MAY INDICATE TRAUMA

Traumatized children may experience both physical and emotional distress. Educators must not assume a child showing signs of trauma will just "get over it". Being an advocate for the child is vital. Without treatment, the damage done by childhood trauma can last a lifetime – with consequences as serious as a risk of suicide that is 15 times higher than the general population. But, with trauma-informed information and interventions, educators can interrupt this impact. The goal is to help move the children who have experienced trauma from victim thinking to survivor thinking. This leads to empowerment, choice, active involvement in their own healing process, and a renewed sense of safety and hope. Educators and school professionals are encouraged to learn about how trauma impacts children so that they are able to provide supports and intervention. This will help minimize the learning and behavioral difficulties that can result when the needs of trauma.

Even if the situation doesn't seem bad to you,
it is how the student feels that matters most.

UNDERSTAND TRAUMA'S IMPACT ACTIVITY

TRAUMA activates the stress response. When the brain stem is activated, do the following physical symptoms increase (▲) or decrease (▼)? Circle the arrow below that applies.

▲	Heart rate	▼
▲	Respiration	▼
▲	Muscle tension	▼
▲	Blood flow	▼
▲	Coritisol	▼
▲	Adrenalin	▼

thinking brain

sensory brain

brain stem

When this activation lasts for LESS than four weeks it is called **acute stress.**

When this activation lasts for MORE than four weeks it is called **postraumatic stress.**

When stressed, the Thinking Brain:

❏ WORKS WELL or ❏ DOES NOT WORK WELL

Name or describe three symptoms of trauma as a result of the stress impact on the Thinking Brain:

1. _____

2. _____

3. _____

When stressed, the Sensory Brain:

❏ WORKS WELL or ❏ DOES NOT WORK WELL

Name or describe three symptoms of trauma as a result of the stress impact on the Sensory Brain:

1. _____

2. _____

3. _____

Students in trauma often react by engaging in fight, flight, or freeze responses.

Describe a student experience for each of the responses in the appropriate boxes below.

FIGHT

FLIGHT

FREEZE

POTENTIAL SIGNS AND SYMPTOMS THAT MAY INDICATE TRAUMA

- Loss of appetite
- Easily startled
- Difficulty concentrating or remembering
- Frequent headaches or stomachaches
- Constant state of alert
- Diminished interest in school and activities
- Inability to experience joy or pleasure
- Self-blame or shame
- Feeling of detachment from others
- Recurrent conflicts with peers
- Irritability
- Outbursts of anger
- Trouble focusing on classwork
- Acting as if the traumatic event was recurring

Trauma is not just the incident itself, but rather how the person experiences what happened or what is happening. Every person will have a unique response to life based upon their past experiences, coping skills, characteristics of resilience, and protective factors. The perception of what has happened or what is happening is more important than the actual event. Adults often assume certain events are more traumatic than others. Adults may also assume that some events are just normal things every kids needs to learn how to "get through". For example, many adults think that teasing from peers is a normal "rite of passage", instead of bullying. We can't assume we know what is traumatizing or not traumatizing to a student. Instead, we need to be curious and ask how that particular event is impacting them.

Try not to judge the trauma. Educators may unintentionally project that a situation isn't really that bad, but how the child feels about the stress is what matters most. Remember, the perception of the child is what matters most. For example, a child who lives in poverty may worry about the family being able to pay rent, find a job, and have enough food to eat. Ongoing stressors can cause trauma reactions — any stress that lasts for longer than 4-6 weeks is post-traumatic stress.

ACTIVITY:
Overlapping Symptomology

When you look at the most common signs and symptoms of post-traumatic stress, what other disorders would you suspect if you just saw symptoms and reactions, and didn't know there was a history of or exposure to trauma?

Examples:

- Re-experiencing the trauma even though it is over

  Psychosis: people don't see or hear the same things I do
  _____

- Marked loss of interest in or participation in significant activities

  Depression
  _____

- Hyper-vigilance

  ADHD
  _____

- Avoidance of traumatic triggers, memories, or reminders of the trauma

  _____

- Negative beliefs about oneself and the world arising from the event

  _____

- Negative emotional state or inability to experience positive emotions

  _____

- Feelings of detachment from people

  _____

- Sleep problems

  _____

- Over-use of alcohol or substance abuse

_____

- Over- or under-eating

_____

- Irritability and angry outbursts

_____

- Reckless or self-destructive behavior

_____

- Exaggerated startle responses

_____

- Concentration problems

_____

If you mentioned that some of the symptoms look like anxiety, depression, substance abuse, eating disorders, bipolar disorder, ADHD, and ODD, you are correct. In fact, because of the overlap in symptomology between trauma and so many other disorders, two experts in the field of childhood trauma have proposed that there be a new diagnosis in for children of trauma called Developmental Trauma Disorder.

DEVELOPMENTAL TRAUMA DISORDER

Because of the abundant research that found traumatized children today are going undiagnosed and misdiagnosed, two leading childhood trauma experts, Robert Pynoos and Bessel van der Kolk, proposed a more relevant trauma category: Developmental Trauma Disorder (DTD). DTD was proposed because it reflects how traumatized children present as well as the abundant documentation neuroscience has provided regarding trauma's impact on the brain, the body, behavior, learning and emotions. Although not included in the DSM-5, the proposed DTD category presents a much more comprehensive, representative, and descriptive view of how traumatized children experience themselves, others, and the world around them as a result of their chronic, intensely stressful lives. DTD remains under consideration, but its contents are relevant to anyone who works with children of trauma. The focus on the subjective experience of trauma is critical to appreciating what matters most in our efforts to best understand and respond to traumatized children.

DIFFERENTIAL DIAGNOSIS BETWEEN TRAUMA, ADHD & ODD

As indicated in the previous activity, the symptoms and responses following trauma or during chronic exposure to stress can look like many other disorders. Two of the most common diagnoses in the school setting for children of all ages are Attention Deficit Hyperactivity Disorder (ADHD) and Oppositional Defiant Disorder (ODD). It is very common for trauma to be mistaken as ADHD or ODD, even by the most well respected and experienced educators. The differential diagnoses isn't easy, but it is helpful to understand how and why this common mistake is made.

The differential diagnoses between trauma, ADHD, and ODD present significant challenges. First, there are several overlapping symptoms of PTSD, ADHD, and ODD. The diagnoses are not mutually exclusive, and there are currently significant assessment limitations.

This reality is terrifying and convicting for many educators. Often, it is the classroom teacher who first suggests the idea that a child may have ADHD, and this suggestion typically results from the child not "fitting into the box" of behavior expected of students in traditional learning environments. Uninformed educators, social workers, parents, and even medical professionals can quickly turn this suggestion into a misdiagnosis if they are not asking the right questions. In the end, a child who has experienced trauma and needs therapy may instead receive medication to treat a condition they do not have. Once professionals see the salient symptoms that PTSD and ADHD share, their common question becomes: "Is it PTSD or ADHD? Both?" Unfortunately, this question is not an easy one to answer.

For example:
- Abused children often exhibit high levels of hyperactivity.
- Inattention is one of the cardinal symptoms of ADHD, but inattention may also be the result of re-experiencing trauma, hypervigilance, and/or the avoidance of stimuli as a result of trauma.

- Research tells us that a history of abuse/early childhood stress are risk factors for future psychopathology, including ADHD, and there is significant research showing a high overlap between ADHD and PTSD in populations of abused children.
- ADHD symptoms occur in 25-45 percent of severely maltreated children, well above the 9 percent rate of ADHD in the general population.
- ADHD is significantly more common among abused children with PTSD (37 percent) than in children without PTSD (17 percent), and physical and sexual abuse are more common in 6-12-year-old girls with ADHD than without ADHD.

It could be trauma, ADHD, or both. This research is why the need of providing a thorough and well-informed assessment before labeling or diagnosing a child is necessary, and is why routine inquiries about trauma histories are strongly recommended (Wilmott, 2008; Briscoe & Hinshaw, 2006; Weinstein, Staffelback & Biassio, 2000).

Overlapping symptoms of both trauma and ADHD include:

ADHD & TRAUMA

HYPERVIGILANCE
INATTENTION
DETACHMENT
IRRITABILITY
ANGER OUTBURSTS
DISTRACTION
RESTLESSNESS
IMPATIENCE
IMPULSIVENESS
DIFFICULTY CONCENTRATING
LIMITED FUTURE ORIENTATION

There are also many overlapping symptoms between trauma and ODD. Children with a history of traumatic experiences exhibit greater oppositional defiant behaviors than children without exposure to trauma. This is most likely the result of the negative physiological impact trauma has on core regulatory systems, compromising a child's ability to regulate and process sensory inputs. Changes in the body's critical stress response system prevent the modulation of sensory deregulation, making the child incapable of self-regulating their emotions and behavior. The experience of trauma increases vulnerability to stressors – even mild stressors that healthy individuals are able to handle. For example, simple problem solving becomes difficult, causing anger and confusion in a child that simply "does not know what to do" about a situation, ultimately resulting in rage, aggression, and other oppositional defiant-like disorders.

Under stress, traumatized children's analytical capacities are limited and behaviorally react with confusion, withdrawal, and/or rage. Rather than making a gradual shift from right brain hemisphere dominance (feeling and sensory) to dominance of the left hemisphere (language, reasoning, problem solving) resulting in an integration of neural communication between hemispheres, they react only from their "sensory" or right brain, often lacking the "thought" or planning before action is taken.

Interestingly, many of the symptoms and reactions present in ODD are parallel to the symptoms and reactions in children post-trauma. More than 800,000 children are exposed to trauma annually from abuse and neglect alone. Twenty percent of those children are observed to have dramatic changes in behavior consistent with ODD following a traumatic event. It would be beneficial to develop guidelines helping pediatricians and other early childhood professionals routinely screen for the presence of trauma-related symptoms and impairments even in very young children. This would prevent the mislabeling of ODD in later years. As one of the top diagnoses given to children today, it is certainly important to understand both the etiology and intervention options proposed for ODD. When ODD is viewed from a biological and trauma-informed perspective, compassion from parents, caregivers, and teachers often follows.

If you look at just the symptoms and the reactions without viewing a student through a trauma-informed lens, it would be easy for even a well-intentioned professional to suspect and misdiagnose a traumatized child as having ADHD or ODD.

ACTIVITY:
Symptoms & Reactions

- How many students in your school building are diagnosed with ADHD? ODD?

_____

- How many of those students also have traumatic history or are experiencing traumatic or toxic stress currently?

_____

- How will what you have learned in Step 2 change your view of these children?

_____

- What will you do about this new knowledge you have related to these students?

_____

Q **How can I support one of my 6th grade students whose grandmother just died? They were very close, and he just can't seem to focus and is so withdrawn that I am worried about him. How should I react?**

What might look like inattention and withdrawal are actually normal grief and trauma reactions. Normalize the reactions by saying, "I get it, it is hard to pay attention with so many other things on your mind. And, you probably don't even feel like socializing or having fun because you feel sad." Give the student permission to put their head down or go into the hallway for a drink of water during the day if they need a break. Let them know that even though they feel sad, it might help to do something with a friend that they enjoy. Referring the child to a counselor, in or outside of the school setting, might be helpful if you still see the student struggling at the 2-month mark after the death.

THE ADVERSE CHILDHOOD EXPERIENCES STUDY

The Adverse Childhood Experiences (ACE) study (Felitti, 2009) is one of the largest investigations ever conducted to assess the associations between adverse childhood experiences and later life health and well-being. More than 17,000 participants were part of this study. The participants were mostly white, college-educated, employed adults who were screened for 10 prominent childhood traumatic experiences as part of their routine healthcare protocol. Each type of trauma was given one point. 70% of participants experienced at least one type of trauma.

ACE scores of 4 or more resulted in four times the risk of emphysema or chronic bronchitis; over four times the likelihood of depression; and 12 times the risk of suicide. ACE scores were directly related with early initiation of smoking, sexual activity, adolescent pregnancy, and risk for intimate partner violence. Findings suggest that certain experiences are major risk factors for the leading causes of illness and death, as well as poor quality of life in the United States.

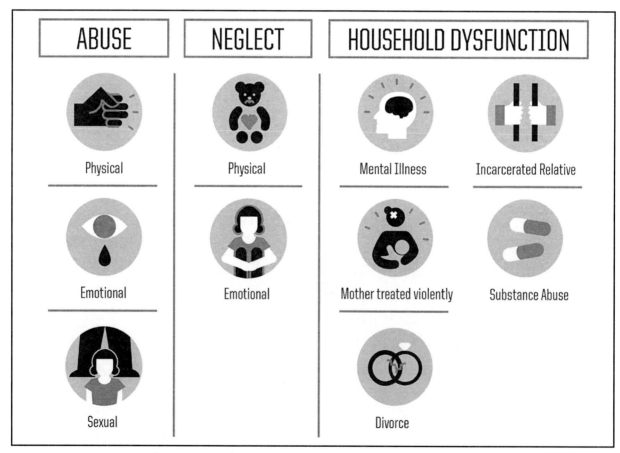

Source: Centers for Disease Control and Prevention
Credit: Robert Wood Johnson Foundation

ACTIVITY:
Adverse Childhood Experiences Questionnaire & Reflection

There are 10 types of childhood trauma measured in the ACE Study. Five are personal — physical abuse, verbal abuse, sexual abuse, physical neglect, and emotional neglect. Five are related to other family members: a parent who's an alcoholic, a mother who's a victim of domestic violence, a family member in jail, a family member diagnosed with a mental illness, and the disappearance of a parent through divorce, death, or abandonment. Each type of trauma counts as one. So a person who's been physically abused, with one alcoholic parent, and a mother who was beaten up has an ACE score of three.

There are, of course, many other types of childhood trauma — watching a sibling being abused, losing a caregiver (grandmother, mother, grandfather, etc.), homelessness, surviving and recovering from a severe accident, witnessing a father being abused by a mother, witnessing a grandmother abusing a father, etc.

The most important thing to remember is that the ACE score is meant as a guideline: If you experienced other types of toxic stress over months or years, then those would likely increase your risk of health consequences. It is also important to keep in mind that characteristics of resilience and exposure to protective factors will mitigate the impact of adversity.

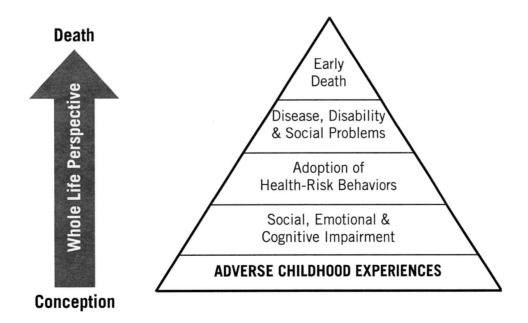

ACE QUESTIONNAIRE

Prior to your 18th birthday:

❐ No ❐ Yes Did a parent or other adult in the household often or very often... swear at you, insult you, put you down, or humiliate you? or act in a way that made you afraid that you might be physically hurt?

❐ No ❐ Yes Did a parent or other adult in the household often or very often... push, grab, slap, or throw something at you? or ever hit you so hard that you had marks or were injured?

❐ No ❐ Yes Did an adult or person at least 5 years older than you ever... touch or fondle you or have you touch their body in a sexual way? or attempt or actually have oral, anal, or vaginal intercourse with you?

❐ No ❐ Yes Did you often or very often feel that ... no one in your family loved you or thought you were important or special? or your family didn't look out for each other, feel close to each other, or support each other?

❐ No ❐ Yes Did you often or very often feel that ... you didn't have enough to eat, had to wear dirty clothes, and had no one to protect you? or your parents were too drunk or high to take care of you or take you to the doctor if you needed it?

❐ No ❐ Yes Were your parents ever separated or divorced?

❐ No ❐ Yes Was your mother or stepmother often or very often pushed, grabbed, slapped, or had something thrown at her? or sometimes, often, or very often kicked, bitten, hit with a fist, or hit with something hard? or ever repeatedly hit over at least a few minutes or threatened with a gun or knife?

❐ No ❐ Yes Did you live with anyone who was a problem drinker or alcoholic, or who used street drugs?

❐ No ❐ Yes Was a household member depressed or mentally ill, or did a household member attempt suicide?

❐ No ❐ Yes Did a household member go to prison?

_____ Add up your "Yes" answers. This is your ACE Score.

Now that you've got your ACE score, what does it mean?

The CDC's Adverse Childhood Experiences Study (ACE Study) uncovered a stunning link between childhood trauma and the chronic diseases people develop as adults, as well as social and emotional problems. This includes heart disease, lung cancer, diabetes, and many autoimmune diseases, as well as depression, violence, being a victim of violence, and suicide.

The study's researchers came up with an ACE score to explain a person's risk for chronic disease. Think of it as a cholesterol score for childhood toxic stress. You get one point for each type of trauma. The higher your ACE score, the higher your risk of health and social problems.

As your ACE score increases, so does the risk of disease, social, and emotional problems. With an ACE score of 4 or more, things start getting serious. The likelihood of chronic pulmonary lung disease increases 390 percent; hepatitis, 240 percent; depression, 460 percent; suicide, 1,220 percent.

ACTIVITY:
Reflection

Reflection questions about your ACE Questionnaire:

- Does anything surprise you about your ACE quiz?

_____

_____

_____

_____

- Did any specific emotion or body sensation come up as you answered the ACE quiz questions?

_____

_____

_____

_____

- When you think about the students in your school, how do you think they would score on the ACE quiz?

_____

_____

_____

Remember this...

- Don't assume – be curious.
- Always wonder what is driving the behavior you see.
- Screen for trauma exposure (past and current).
- Trauma is something we experience at a sensory, not a cognitive, level.
- Trauma-informed interventions can interrupt the impact trauma has on children.

A NOTE ABOUT STEPS 3, 4, 5, AND 6.

The next four steps are proactive strategies, and are beneficial for every student in your classroom and school – both students who have experienced trauma and for those who have not. These strategies will lower stress and they will foster and nurture characteristics of resilience. The concepts you will learn in these steps are the foundation for implementing tier one supports for all students at every age. When steps 3, 4, 5, and 6 are implemented with 100% fidelity, every day, there is rarely a need for supports at the tier 2 or 3 levels. As you know, in every school, there will always be a small percentage of students who will require tier 2 and 3 supports, even when tier 1 supports are in consistently in place.

STEP 3

Foster Connections

School connectedness is a significant protective factor for all students regardless of race, ethnic group, or level of family income. The U.S. Centers for Disease Control and Prevention (CDC) conducted a national study of 36,000 7th to 12th grade students. School connectedness was indicated as the strongest factor for both boys and girls in preventing substance abuse, violence, and absenteeism. School connectedness was the second-most important factor (after family) in helping students avoid suicide, emotional problems, and eating disorders. Students who feel connected to their school are also more likely to have better academic achievement, including higher grades and test scores; have better school attendance; and stay in school longer.

Children who report feeling connected to their school are more likely to succeed and less likely to exhibit disruptive or violent behavior, carry/use a weapon, consider or attempt suicide, smoke, use drugs and alcohol, and be emotionally distressed. School connectedness is the belief held by students that adults or peers in their school care about their learning, as well as them as individuals.

Bonds with caring adults provide children with warmth, security, and meaningful interactions. Indicators of a society's health are positively related to interconnectedness, and most risk factors decline in the face of strong connections. Being given opportunities to explore new actions, activities, and relationships with adults who keep the child safe build the foundation for developing resilience.

ADULT SUPPORT

School staff can dedicate their time, interest, attention, and emotional support to students to build connections. Children learn from "green light" people – staff they experience as safe. Taking the time to foster connections sets students up to do well both academically and in their interactions with others.

Connections are made in the ongoing and repetitive moment to moment interactions school professionals have with students. Think of making connections like a game of tennis. "Serve and return" interactions help foster connections. When a student makes a signal to an adult in school, and that adult is informed and responsive to the student's signal and need, they are providing an environment rich in "serve and return" experiences. If an adult's responses to a student's signal are inconsistent or absent, the serve and return interaction creates a disconnect between the adult and student.

When school professionals have access to trauma-informed training, it can help strengthen the environment of relationships essential to children's lifelong learning, health, and behavior. A breakdown in reciprocal serve and return interactions between adults and children in the school setting can be the result of many factors, such as not understanding how trauma impacts behavior, misreading non-verbal cues, and overstressed staff and students. It is important to emphasize that an adult may have to make several bids to connect (or serves) before a student responds. This is certainly normal with traumatized children who haven't ever experienced an adult in their lives that they can trust or count on. When this happens, professionals need to be patient and continue to make attempts to connect with students. These attempts can be subtle, and may come in the form of a hello, a smile, a question asked about how they are – just noticing the student is a bid to connect. In time, most students – even the most traumatized – will respond to an adult who doesn't give up on them. Another common problem is that an adult will try to respond to a signal that a student provides, only to get it "wrong". If this happens, even though they get it wrong, the student will see that the adult tried. Sometimes we miss the ball with our racket – ask the student how you can best help and try again.

When an infant is crying, a caring adult will try many strategies to soothe the infant. The same needs to happen with older children. Continue to try until you find what works best.

HOW CAN YOU MAKE BIDS TO CONNECT?
5:1 Interactions (Noticing)

While negative interactions are never encouraged, we understand that they happen from time to time. The goal is to increase the number of positive interactions with students over negative interactions. The critical ratio is 5:1. Just by noticing a student, you are engaging in a positive interaction. Positive interactions and noticing occur when you engage in friendly conversation, provide non-verbal acknowledgment like a head nod, wave or smile, offer praise for something done well, and offer support when you see a child struggling. Negative interactions examples include criticism, punishment, and negative or non-existent non-verbal acknowledgment.

5:1 interactions increase connections → students feel engaged → motivation increases → academic achievement and regulated behavior improves

---

Examples of how to provide positive interactions:

- Praise for correct answers (e.g., "You worked really hard on that one!")
- Appreciation for assignments turned in or work completed (e.g., "Thank you for getting your homework turned in – great work!")
- Acknowledgment of character strengths (e.g., "That took a lot of courage to try that difficult question."
- Positive greetings (e.g., "Good morning, we missed you yesterday and I'm happy you're feeling better today!")
- Gratitude for good behavior (e.g., "Thank you so much for helping clear up the paper scraps.")
- Take a moment to check in with a student (e.g., "How is your family?")
- Inquiring about hobbies or interests (e.g., "I heard your track team had a meet yesterday, how did you do?")
- Smile or give friendly gestures like a fist pump or wave.

Every interaction we have with a student matters. This is because our brains have something called mirror neurons. A mirror neuron is a neuron that fires both when a person acts and when a person observes the same action performed by another. Thus, the neuron "mirrors" the behavior of the other, as though the observer were itself acting. In other words, neurons tune into the emotions of others. We tend to mimic and match moods, facial expressions, and behavior as empathy. This is the basis of not just mutual hostility, but also friendly interactions. For staff working with youth who exhibit problematic behavior, this can become a pitfall or be used as a powerful tool. For example, think of a student who is acting in an aggressive manner. If the adult who is responding to the student begins charging toward the student, raising their voice, and widely opening their eyes, this will often further escalate the student because their mirror neurons will respond accordingly. However, if the adult responds calmly, with an even tone of voice and non-threatening body posture, the student's central nervous system will begin to de-escalate.

CLASSROOM MEETINGS

We can't say enough about the benefit of classroom meetings. Classroom meetings build community and are a great way to implement the concepts you will learn in the additional steps in this book.

How to Implement a Classroom Meeting

Step 1

Form a circle (safely and quickly). Teacher and students discuss, decide, and practice:

- Floor or chairs
- Where, how do you get there?
- Who do you sit by?
- What does it look like?
- What does it sound like?

Step 2

Introduce the talking piece (only the person holding the talking piece may talk). A talking piece can be a small toy, a special stick or stone, or some other object that can withstand being passed around the room multiple times.

Circles are characterized by the use of a talking piece, which regulates communication. Both talking and listening are important in the circle because mutual understanding lays the groundwork for deeper, more meaningful discussion. Only participants holding the talking piece can talk. Participants who do not have the talking piece get to listen and reflect on what the person with the talking piece says. Receiving the talking piece is an invitation to share with the group and helps ensure that everyone gets an opportunity to share at their own pace and in their own way without interruptions. Participants share what they want, can remain silent during their turn, or pass by giving the talking piece to the next person. The talking piece is passed clockwise around the circle with each participant having a turn to share their authentic personal stories and have them respectfully heard and acknowledged without judgment, condemnation, or advice (unless advice is solicited).

Step 3

Practice using various topics to create proactive classroom meetings. A typical classroom meeting will include any one or more of the topics listed below.

Classroom Meeting Topics:

Get to Know You and Greetings

One minute greeting. Set a timer for one minute and students try to greet each other using a verbal greeting including the person's name, a smile, eye contact, and a handshake or hug. This activity helps to create a sense of belonging in your classroom.

Who Am I

Write a "Who Am I? Riddle". Students write four or five statements about themselves followed by the last line, the question "Who Am I?" Then, put the students' riddles up as a bulletin board and let students guess each person. The first person to guess correctly gets to choose who guesses next.

Compliments and Appreciations

Compliments and appreciations are a good way to build in recognitions, making sure no one is left out and everyone's strengths are noticed and appreciated. Discuss what a true compliment is. "I appreciated it when you...thank you for...I noticed you...That really helped me when..."

Encourage students to focus on actions rather than things you like about another person's appearance. For example, "I noticed how you did your hair a different way today. How did you do that?" rather than saying, "I like your hair." Be careful of backhanded compliments. "Thanks for not hitting me today like you usually do." One option with this topic is to offer students a choice of giving or getting a compliment. Encourage students to notice and appreciate each other during the school day so they can give a compliment at the next classroom meeting.

Practice Speaking and Listening in Natural Settings

While speaking and listening are vital in the classroom, they are useful in all areas of students' lives. Start by having students talk about their interests, then role play situations they might encounter, such as an argument with a friend or how to respectfully disagree with someone in a position of authority.

Turn Taking

Use an object, such as a talking piece as a signal for turn-taking. Teach your students that when they have the object, it is their turn to talk or pass and others are expected to listen.

Universal Needs

Talk to students about the Circle of Courage® and the four universal needs of belonging, mastery, independence, generosity:

- What does each universal need look like?
- Create posters, skits, or charts with your students displaying each need.
- What happens when one of the universal needs is not met?
- Say, "We will be helping each other make sure our needs are met. When you understand that people will get their needs met in whatever ways they can, it helps us to teach them how to meet their needs in healthy ways. What are some ways we can get our needs met in the classroom?"
- Talk about how characters in books or in history act when their needs are met or are not met.

You can also use classroom meeting time for problem solving, learning about differences, reviewing class content, preparing for tests or quizzes, restorative practices, teaching emotional awareness and regulation, practicing relationships skills, as well as many other topics that come up in your classroom.

SPOTLIGHT: DR. RITA PIERSON, EDUCATOR

Dr. Rita Pierson was an educator for more than 40 years, serving as a teacher, special education teacher, counselor, assistant principal, director, testing coordinator, and consultant. She is probably best remembered for her inspirational advocacy that positive human connection (relationship) is the key to education.

Her famous quotes: "Kids don't learn from people they don't like" and "Every child deserves a champion; an adult who will never give up on them, who understands the power of connection and insists that they become the best they can possibly be" have been used as rallying cries for those in the education field who understand that building caring relationships with students and fostering resilience are the most important things a teacher can do, and that learning will not take place unless this is happening.

Using a student's name often will foster a connection between you and the student.

ACTIVITY:
Connections Assessment

- First, either list the names or place photographs of every child in your school, grade, or classroom on the walls of the school cafeteria or gymnasium.

- Then, invite all staff members (not only teachers) and consistent parent helpers to walk around the room and place a sticker or check mark next to every child's name or photograph with whom they feel they have a connection.

- Afterward, identify kids who are without connections or have little connections and assign a few staff members to each of these children. Encourage staff to make a point to say hello and greet these kids as often as they can during the school year. Almost every day is ideal. The goal is to make every child feel like an adult, or several adults, notice them and are excited to see them in class, in the hallway, or at school events. The kids with little or no adult connections are the ones who need connections most. The caring adults in your school are the perfect people to help increase the overall school connectedness that children experience.

This is a powerful and effective way to ensure every student in your building feels connected and like they belong.

CASE EXAMPLE:
LUKE FOSTERING CONNECTIONS THROUGH GENEROSITY

Luke transferred to his school right after Christmas break. All that Luke's teacher knew about him was that he recently moved from another state. His hair hung in his face and he never smiled at anyone. He completed his assignments and didn't cause any trouble in the classroom, but he never looked happy. When she asked him a question, he would usually shrug his shoulders and not answer. When he did answer, the answer was short. The other students didn't dislike Luke, but they gave up trying to engage him. After a few days of asking him to play and him not responding, they just left him alone. After attending a trauma-informed school training, Luke's teacher was determined to connect with him. She tried to make a list of everything she did know about him. She could think of two things:

- He seemed to be catching on really well to fractions.
- He always wore a hat with the same sports team logo on it.

The next week when she saw Luke, she asked him if he would be willing to be paired up with another student during math who was having a hard time with fractions. He didn't say yes, but he didn't say no either, so during their math lesson she paired up all of the students. Luke was paired with Tony. She watched them carefully. For the first few minutes they worked side by side, not together. But then she noticed that Tony was starting to get frustrated and Luke quickly intervened. For what seemed like the first time, she heard Luke's voice, "Oh here's a trick my brother taught me about multiplying fractions." Tony's eyes lit up. She had the boys work together during math for the next few days. On day 3, she overheard them talking about a basketball game they had both watched over the weekend. They were connecting!

In time, Tony and Luke began to play basketball together at recess and it looked like they were developing a nice friendship. They even started to make plans to get together after school and on the weekend with other boys to play basketball.

The teacher learned at 2nd marking period conferences that Luke's older brother was killed in a car accident before they moved. Luke's mother told his teacher that the family needed a fresh start and that is why they had moved. Luke and his brother were close in age and the best of friends. Luke's mother reported that he was sad and withdrawn, until one day he came home "a little bit happier." When she asked him why he seemed more upbeat that day he said, "I taught someone something that Chris taught me — I remembered and it helped the other kid."

By March of that school year, Luke was like a different kid. He was talkative, smiled more, and was planning to attend a basketball day camp with Tony over the summer.

Belonging to a Positive Peer Group

A stable network of peers can improve student perceptions of school. Peer support is a type of social support provided by one's peers. While a person's 'peer group' is usually taken to mean other people of similar age or gender, individuals may also identify their peers according to shared interests, issues, life experiences, or personal attributes. Adolescents increasingly turn to their peers (if available) for social and emotional support during periods of conflict, confusion, and help-seeking. Access to social support has been identified as a protective factor for well-being.

Educators should lead plenty of discussions about individual interests and experiences so that students have a better understanding of each other. Facilitating a guided conversation during classroom meetings with students to help them recognize similarities and differences they may have with the peer group can add to feelings of social support.

SCHOOL BELONGING	
Positive Health Impact	Positive Academic Impact
—DECREASED—	—INCREASED—
Substance Abuse	Self Efficacy
Early Sexual Initiation	Motivation
Violence	Attendance
Suicidal Ideation	Persistance
Eating Disorders	Achievement

ACTIVITY:
Who I Am

There are many variations of the "Who I Am" activity. You can use the one we have included on page 69, or you can have students create a poster, a poem, a slide show, a "top ten" list, etc. to describe themselves. It can be helpful to give students sentence starters, like those below, to spur their thinking and writing.

- **I love** _____ **because** _____

- **I wonder** _____

- **I am happy when** _____

- **I am scared when** _____

- **I worry about** _____ **because** _____

- **I hope to** _____

- **I am sad when** _____

- **In the future, I will** _____

Students could share their projects to the entire class or in small groups.

ACTIVITY:
Peer Interviews

This activity will help students get to know each other.

Ask the following questions to your peer. Write down their answers.

Who is your hero?

What is your favorite kind of book to read?

What or who makes you laugh the most?

Do you have a nickname? What is it?

What is your favorite holiday? Why is it your favorite?

Do you collect anything? If not, what do you think would be interesting to collect?

Who knows you the best?

ACTIVITY:
Teacher Interviews

This activity encourages student-teacher interaction and connection.

Ask the following questions to your teacher. Write down their answers.

Who is your hero?

What is your favorite kind of book to read?

What or who makes you laugh the most?

Do you have a nickname? What is it?

What is your favorite holiday? Why is it your favorite?

Do you collect anything? If not, what do you think would be interesting to collect?

Who knows you the best?

ACTIVITY:
Who I Am

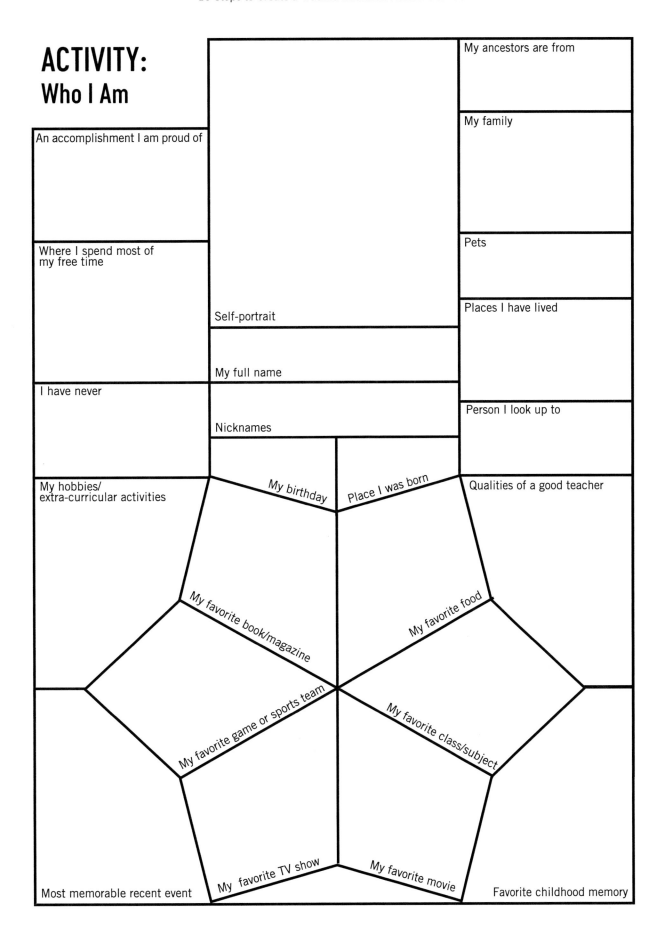

My ancestors are from

My family

Pets

Places I have lived

Person I look up to

An accomplishment I am proud of

Where I spend most of my free time

I have never

My hobbies/ extra-curricular activities

Self-portrait

My full name

Nicknames

My birthday

Place I was born

Qualities of a good teacher

My favorite book/magazine

My favorite food

My favorite game or sports team

My favorite class/subject

Most memorable recent event

My favorite TV show

My favorite movie

Favorite childhood memory

At-risk youth who lack a supportive peer group can feel socially isolated and are at higher risk of developing mental health problems including depression, anxiety, and suicidal ideation (Lobo et al, 2010). Creating peer support groups of at-risk youth can be beneficial because it provides access to supportive peers facing similar issues and concerns.

 **I have a 5th grader who has been placed in three different foster homes in the past year. What can I do to help him stay on track? His home life is so unstable, and I can see it is affecting him at school too.**

The best thing you can do is be a constant, stable person in his world. Since you don't have control of what goes on outside of your classroom, focus on what you can control. Create a routine that provides him with consistency and predictability. And, remember, to have one consistent, caring adult in the life of a child – even if it isn't a caregiver or parent – is one of the most beneficial characteristics of building resilience.

Remember this...

STEP 3 HIGHLIGHTS

- Of all of the steps, some say this is the most important one. Foster connections! Make sure that every student feels connected in their school to both adults and their peers.
- Conduct a school-wide connections assessment.
- Hold daily classroom meetings.

STEP 4

Prioritize Social and Emotional Skill Development

Trauma-informed resilient schools prioritize the connection between social and emotional skills and optimal school success for students. Schools must focus on more than standardized tests and academic achievements. For many children, especially those living in poverty, school is their only true socialization environment. For the past two decades, there has been growing interest in examining the connection between social emotional functioning and academic achievement. School-based social emotional learning programs are intimately linked to improving children's academic performance (Jones & Bouffard, 2012). Children participating in social emotional learning programs demonstrate improvements in multiple areas including:

- Enhanced social and emotional skills.
- Improved attitudes towards self, school, and others.
- Enhanced positive social behavior.
- Reduced conduct problems (misbehavior and aggression).
- Reduced emotional distress (stress and depression).
- Improved academic performance (test scores and school grades).

Although some educators argue against implementing this type of programming because it takes valuable time away from core academic material, the findings suggest social and emotional learning does not distract from academic performance and actually increases students' performance on standardized tests and grades.

We've been talking about emotions for years, but the science of emotions is new. Many schools simply haven't made the connection between emotions and learning. This isn't because schools don't care – it is only because they haven't learned why or how to prioritize social and emotional skills. Not being given the opportunity and guidance to enhance social and emotional learning leaves a child with only a fraction of what is needed to grow and prosper.

Difficulty regulating emotions can lead to a host of problems in the school setting. Deficits in the capacity to regulate emotion are cause for serious concern because the ability to modulate behavior, attention, and emotions are the foundation for children's adaptive functioning in three key domains: self-development, academic achievement, and interpersonal relationships (Zins et al, 2004).

A common critique of emphasizing social and emotional curricula is the time and energy on social and behavioral goals at the expense of learning. Education has become increasingly accountable for raising academic standards through measures such as standardized tests in the core curriculum areas. Many educators find themselves under increased pressure to meet external requirements, with the reduction in curriculum time for subjects where little accountability is required is frequently undermined. Now, more than ever, it is important for social and emotional skill curricula to demonstrate their impact on academic performance.

Social and emotional learning is defined as the process through which we recognize and manage our own emotions. Emotional awareness and regulation are the cornerstones of social and emotional competence. Trauma-informed resilient schools realize how intimately connected learning social and emotional skills are with moving a traumatized child from victim to survivor thinking.

EMOTIONAL AWARENESS

Emotional awareness is the ability to accurately recognize one's emotions and thoughts and their influence on behavior. Learning how to be emotionally aware and recognizing the sensations felt within your body is one of the most important steps in healing from toxic stress and trauma. However, all students need to learn how to recognize what is happening in their bodies – the sensations they experience with various feelings - if we want them to better manage their emotions, especially those that are overwhelming. More time should be spent practicing emotional awareness with students. All too often, educators move to teaching and expecting emotional regulation from students. Emotional awareness is essential. Without it, emotional regulation is difficult. Many would even argue that without emotional awareness, emotional regulation is impossible.

Co-Regulation

Adults play a critical role in shaping and supporting self-regulation in an interactive process called "co-regulation". Self-regulation develops through interaction with caregivers such as parents, teachers, coaches, and other mentors. It is dependent upon predictable, responsive, and supportive environments. Regardless of their role, a caring adult's warmth, responsiveness, and sensitivity support self-regulation development and may buffer the effects of toxic stress and trauma. Co-regulation will look different at all ages as the capacity for self-regulation grows, but remains a critical resource across development – especially for children who didn't experience such in their early years.

The three broad categories of support that adults can provide to children that will help them develop foundational self-regulatory skills, and expand these skills to meet increasingly complex regulatory needs at they grow include (Murray et al., 2015):

1. Provide a warm, responsive relationship by displaying care and affection; recognizing and responding to cues that signal needs and wants; and providing support in times of stress.

2. Structure the environment to make self-regulation manageable, providing a buffer against environmental stressors. This means creating an environment that is physically and emotionally safe for children to explore and learn at their level of development. Consistent, predictable routines and expectations promote a sense of security by providing clear goals for regulation.

3. Teach and coach self-regulation skills through modeling, instruction, opportunities for practice, prompts for enactment, and reinforcement of each step toward successful use of skills. Teach skills, provide support, and scaffolding for self-regulation enactment in the moment.

Co-Regulation for Elementary-Aged Children

Elementary age children gain more control over their attention, emotions, and behavior and have a growing ability to manage their impulses, delay gratification, and become aware of their own thoughts. At the same time, behavioral expectations and social interactions in the school environment become more complex. It is important to remember developmental versus chronological age when working with children who experience trauma and toxic stress. A student in the 3rd grade may chronologically be age 8 years old. However, depending upon stress and trauma histories, their developmental age may be closer to 5 or 6 years old requiring added co-regulation.

- Continue to provide a warm, nurturing, supportive relationship.
- Assist in problem-solving more complex academic, behavioral, and social situations.
- Model conflict resolution strategies.
- Prompt and coach coping skills and calm-down strategies, including self-talk and relaxation.
- Teach and support organization and planning skills needed for academic success.
- Provide opportunities to make decisions and self-monitor behavior.
- Continue to provide clear rules, structure, and consequences in a calm manner.

Co-Regulation for Adolescents

During adolescence, brain development is undergoing major changes that bring both benefits and challenges for self-regulation. For example, brain systems that process emotions and seek rewards are more developed than the cognitive control systems responsible for good decision-making and future planning. This means that teens are often biased towards choices that offer short-term reward rather than long-term benefit, and their emotions heavily influence their decisions. Given that poor decisions during adolescence can have long-term negative consequences, this is not the time to step back from support. Co-regulation during this developmental period is crucial. Though adolescences are separating from caregivers and seeking more independence, maintenance of a warm and accepting relationship with a caring adult is as important as ever. Adolescents need educators and other child-caring practitioners who can listen supportively in times of strong emotion, provide space, and support for youth to calm down in times of conflict and coach coping skills for a multitude of stressful situations. Likewise, though adolescents do need opportunities for independent decision-making and action, they have equal need for caregivers to monitor their actions, protect them from dangerous situations, and support responsible choices.

- Provide a warm, responsive relationship.
- Provide support and empathy in times of intense emotion.
- Model, monitor, and coach more sophisticated self-regulation skills across different contexts.
- Monitor and limit opportunities for risk-taking behavior.
- Provide opportunities to make decisions and self-monitor behavior in less risky situations.
- Give time and space to calm down in times of conflict.
- Monitor and prompt use of organizational and planning skills for successful task completion.
- Continue clear rules, boundaries, and consequences to incentivize good choices.

Your Own Regulation

To co-regulate successfully, adults will need to assess their own capacity for self-regulation.

- Pay attention to feelings and reactions during stressful interactions with a child.
- Pay attention to thoughts and beliefs about the behaviors of others.
- Use strategies to self-calm and respond effectively and compassionately. Adults greatly benefit when taking a moment for some deep breaths and calming self-talk.

Step 9 will provide you with more information about becoming aware of your own capacity to self-regulate and supports that may benefit you.

ACTIVITY:
Feelings and Sensations

Look at each of the feelings listed below and imagine how your body feels when you experience each feeling. For example, when you feel hurt, which part(s) of your body experiences the hurt? Once you identify the body part(s) that experience the feeling, try to determine what the specific sensation is that you experience in that body part with each feeling. For example, if you experience the feeling of hurt in your eyes and chest, how do you know? Maybe when you feel hurt your eyes get tired and heavy, and your chest has a dark and sinking sensation. Use the table of sensation descriptors to help you describe each sensation if you are having trouble finding words to describe the sensation for each feeling.

SENSATIONS CHART

• DENSE	• FLOWING	• QUEASY
• NUMB	• TIGHT	• LIGHT
• WOODEN	• SUFFOCATING	• BLOCKED
• BREATHLESS	• FLUTTERY	• HEAVY
• FULL	• HOT	• COLD
• SWEATY	• KNOTTED	• FAST
• THICK	• NERVOUS	• ELECTRIC
• SPACEY	• ICY	• HOLLOW
• TINGLY	• ENERGIZED	• CALM

(Levine, 2008)

FEELING?	WHERE DO YOU FEEL IT IN YOUR BODY?	WHAT SENSATION DO YOU FEEL?
HURT	CHEST/HEART	HEAVY/DEEP
HAPPY		
WORRY		
ANGRY		
RELAXED		
CONFUSED		
GUILTY		
EXCITED		
EMBARRASSED		
SAD		
SCARED		
BORED		

NOTE: The most common themes of trauma are worry, hurt, fear, anger, guilt, and feeling like a victim. Starr's *One Minute Interventions*, *More One Minute Interventions*, and *Mind Body Skills for Emotional Regulation* are excellent resources to use with students when you are teaching emotional awareness and regulation.

A simple body scan is an excellent tool for educators to use with students to help them gain more emotional awareness. Simply asking the student to point to or color in the area of the body outline where they are most experiencing emotions (anger, hurt, fear) will help bring awareness to their current experience. You can take that a step further by asking them to identify words that describe the sensations they experience in each body part associated with their identified feeling(s).

BODY SCAN

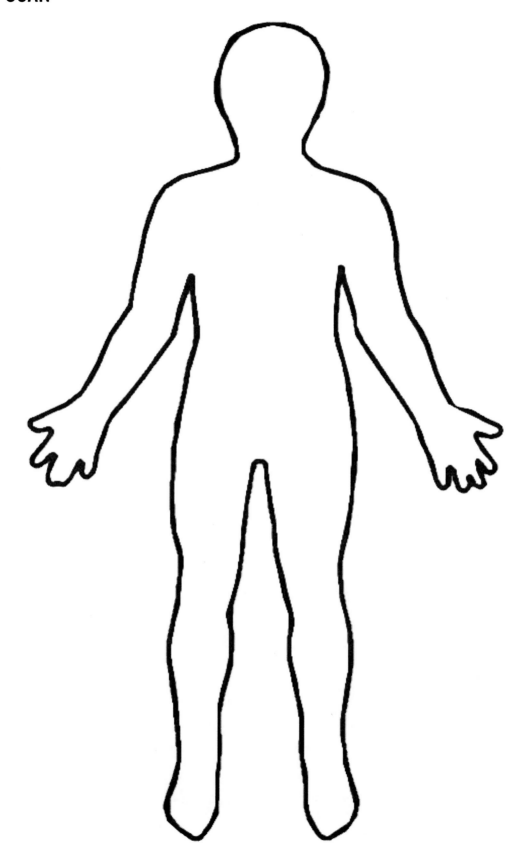

Emotional Regulation

Emotional regulation is the ability to regulate one's emotions, thoughts, and behaviors effectively in different situations. This includes managing stress, controlling impulses, motivating one's self, and setting and working toward personal and academic goals. Emotional regulation is learned when students have opportunities to practice emotional awareness, followed by coping strategies and emotional regulation (even when not overwhelmed). This repeated practice helps them respond better when they are presented with an overwhelming experience. Educators should understand that any decrease in frequency, duration, or intensity of unwanted behaviors is not only progress, but also success.

ACTIVITY:
Emotional Regulation Reflection

- Select a feeling from the list on page 77 that you find challenging to manage.

_____

- How do you usually respond when you experience this feeling?

_____

- Do you behave in a certain way?

_____

- What usually makes this feeling worse?

_____

- What usually makes this feeling better?

_____

- How does the sensation of this feeling change when it feels worse?

_____

- How does the sensation change when it feels better?

_____

- What do your answers to these questions tell you about the feeling, the sensation, and how you respond?

_____

CASE EXAMPLE: JOHN

John is mad. He knows he is mad because he just punched a hole into the wall. He believes he just punched a hole into the wall because a classmate laughed at him for missing every shot he made on the basketball court. John doesn't know how his body feels when he is mad. When asked, he responds, "When I am mad, I feel mad and I need to punch something."

Does this sound familiar? Every feeling has an attached, unique body sensation. For example, the emotion of anger or "mad" may be sensed in the body as a tight and clenched jaw, a racing heart, or arm muscles that are ready to explode. Regardless of what is causing the emotion, identifying body signals is where we should focus our attention. There is a bit of a pause between becoming aware of body signals and our reactions to them. The body message is the sensation that helps us name our emotion – from there we react. As trauma-informed adults, we should spend time practicing body awareness with children before moving into regulation strategies.

After some exploration with John, he identifies muscle tightness and a need to move in his arms and hands when he gets mad. He experiences the same body sensation when he doesn't understand his math homework or when his grandmother repeatedly nags him. John says he has broken a few things that didn't belong to him over the past year both at home and school. John has connected his body sensation to the emotion of anger. John now understands it wasn't the taunting of his peer that resulted in punching the wall — that reaction was driven by the intense energy he needed to release from his arms and hands.

A child will not be able to regulate overwhelming emotions until they know which body sensations are attached to those emotions. Only then can they match an emotional regulation strategy to their body's message and a need to discharge the energy surrounding that emotion. This, however, isn't the final step. Emotional regulation strategies must be practiced with the child when they are both calm and when they are experiencing intense emotions. The ability to take advantage of the pause between the sensation and reaction only comes after awareness and repetitive regulation of that sensation.

John is mad. He knows he is mad because he can feel his arm and hand muscles beginning to tighten and having an urge to move. John knows how his body feels when he is mad. John notices the signal and takes advantage of the pause. Instead of finding himself in the middle of a destructive reaction, he engages in a strategy he has practiced several times over the past few weeks. John walks away and he places his hands up against a wall and imagines pushing that wall with all of his might, slowly releasing the anger energy out of his arms and hands without breaking anything. John knows that it is okay to be angry but it is not okay to break things or destroy property.

Social emotional learning interventions and skill development should be taught within a supportive learning environment, and should also contribute to the enhancement of such a climate. The result will be positive child development and greater attachment and engagement in school. The final outcome is improved academic performance and school success (Zins et al, 2004). Students with well-developed social and emotional skills will be able to "agree" with the following statements about themselves:

- I'm comfortable sharing my feelings.
- I can control my behavior when I am angry, frustrated, disappointed, or excited.
- I notice when others are upset.
- I work well with others.
- I know the difference between right and wrong.
- I can stay focused on tasks even if I don't like them.
- I try to understand how others feel and think.
- I know how to disagree without starting an argument.
- When I make a decision, I think about what might happen afterward.

 **We had a 14-year-old girl in our school commit suicide, and everyone is in shock. How can I help my students get through this? This is the second suicide of a young girl this year.**

It can be very upsetting for both teachers and students when a student commits suicide. There is a lot of concern that talking about suicide and how it happened will lead to "contagion"—making other kids do it—but there is no research to back up that worry. For many kids, it's the opposite, and for them, it's better to talk about the situation. But remember that reactions vary. The event will be very upsetting to some of your students and not to others. We have to respect all symptoms and reactions. There is a continuum, and everyone is going to be on a different page. Schools can offer an outlet for kids who are having the hardest time to come together to process the event, but no one should be required to talk about it. Make it optional. It's best, too, that memorials—for any death—take place outside of school for the same reason. Students should have the choice to participate. It has nothing to do with disrespecting the family or not caring, but it has everything to do with respecting everybody else. When you respect and honor each student's individual reactions, you help create a supportive environment that allows everyone to process and heal in their own way.

RELATIONSHIP SKILLS

As we learned in Step 3, some children's only form of socialization, especially those living in poverty, is school. For those who didn't have early childhood socialization, they may have never learned social and relationship skills.

Benefits

- Interpersonal skills are an important part of students' development.
- Improves self-esteem.
- Increases student buy-in.
- Creates a more cohesive class and group.
- Helps students help one another.
- Increases instructional time.
- Decreases time spent repeating directions, rehashing lessons, etc.
- Improves students' moods, affect, and emotional stability.
- Helps students to interact with adults.
- Helps students to elicit help from teachers and others.
- Teaches students important life skills for dealing with others.
- Reduces conflicts, arguing, and fighting.
- Improves the environment of the room/school.
- Helps students make and keep friends.
- Improves coping skills.
- Increases self-confidence.

Help provide opportunities to build relationship skills.

- Teach lessons on relationships, friendships, getting along with others, tolerance, etc.
- Take students aside to discuss and have them reflect on how their behaviors affect others, what behaviors would make others want to be friends with them, etc.
- Have students partner up and work on projects together.
- Assign work partners.
- Help students set goals with making friends or getting to know others.

HOW TO BE A GOOD FRIEND
To have good friends, you must be a good friend. Here are some of the ways good friends treat each other:

- Good friends listen to each other.
- Good friends don't put each other down or hurt each other's feelings.
- Good friends try to understand each other's feelings and moods.
- Good friends help each other solve problems.
- Good friends give each other compliments.
- Good friends can disagree without hurting each other.
- Good friends are dependable.
- Good friends respect each other.
- Good friends are trustworthy.
- Good friends give each other room to change.

Use this as a guide during one or more of your classroom meetings. Rich discussion can follow when presenting the characteristics of how to be a good friend to students of all ages.

CALMING CORNERS

Design some small areas where a student can retreat and feel calm. Quiet writing alcoves, a cozy bean-bag chair for reading, or a snug "cave" made from a tablecloth and a low table or desk provide for comfortable private areas. Providing a calm-down or comfort spot where angry, frustrated students can go to gain control or students who need time away from the group can feel secure is helpful. Add a bin of fidget toys or other stimulating comfort items like paper and markers, books, headphones and music, or stuffed animals to provide comfortable personal spaces for students.

Tips for implementing the use of comfort corners:

- Use as an opportunity and not a demand.
- Not a consequence.
- A place for comfort and to regain control or take a few minutes away from the class.
- Offer some privacy – yet maintain eye contact with teacher.
- Introduce kids to it – let them try it out before they become upset.

Items you may use to create a comfort/calm down spot

- Pillows and cushions
- Bubble machines
- Bean bags
- Headphones
- Sand tray, ice tray
- Rocking chair
- Puzzles

- Exercise balls
- Sound machines
- Fidget toys
- Sunglasses
- Mini-trampoline
- Coloring supplies

- Weighted blankets/animals
- Lava lamps
- Ear mufflers
- Fish tank
- Swings
- Play-doh, modeling clay

Calm down and comfort spots result in improved mood, fewer disruptive behaviors, decreased anxiety and fear, improved communication, and enhanced interpersonal interactions.

> Kids who have experienced trauma aren't trying to push your buttons. If a child is having trouble with following directions, the student may be distracted because of a situation at home that is causing them to worry. Instead of reprimanding a student for being late or forgetting homework, be affirming and accommodating.

Purpose of a Calming Corner

A calming corner is a small, designated space located within a classroom. The purpose of a calming corner is to help support self-regulation while keeping students in the classroom if they need a break from instruction time or a group activity. The use of calming corners can transform the culture of the classroom because calming corners are not consequence-based, but rather used as an opportunity, driven by a student's choice to feel better. Calming corners are private enough to allow the student to maintain dignity. However, they should be within eyesight of the educator so the student maintains a feeling of safety.

When students experience stress or trauma at home, or are overwhelmed in school, their nervous systems respond. Some students become extremely activated while others shutdown. Activation comes in reactions such as inattention, difficulty sitting still, and hyperactivity. Shutdown looks like daydreaming, falling asleep in class, and not responding to others bids to connect. With both activation and shutdown, cognition is impaired and learning is difficult. Calming corners can help with both. When activated, a calming corner provides an opportunity for students to reset or re-regulate. When shut down, a calming corner provides opportunity for engagement.

Teachers should introduce calming corners in their classrooms as safe places. They are not for students who are "in trouble," but rather for all students in the classroom. Invite all students to "try out" the calming corner when it is implemented. At first, the calming corner will be a novelty and every student will want to try it out. This is normal. As time goes on, only the students who really need to use it will ask to do so. If there is more than one student who wants to use the calming corner, the use of timers is helpful. Typically, after 5 minutes in the calming corner, students are ready to join the rest of the class.

A calming corner can be a safe place for students to do peer-led Restorative Circles or to just process through issues. Classrooms can create calming corner passes or a simple signal individualized by each student to alert the teacher that the student needs to process or calm down.

For school-age children, a small nook or space set apart from the rest of the room that offers privacy is perfect. Provide seating with beanbags, pillows, or a small table and chairs. Some teachers use a tapestry or some sort of "roof" to cover the calming corner space. Peaceful lighting and colors are a bonus. Be sure to post the purpose of the calming corner. As children enter middle school and high school, a small area with a desk, beanbag, or comfortable chair will do the trick. Some like to call these areas "chill-out zones".

"My favorite is when a students go to the comfort corner and other students go back to comfort them or talk through something that is bothering them. In one kindergarten classroom, Joey, who was very aggressive with peers, used the comfort corner to help calm down when he was mad. He hugged the stuffed animals and looked at books. His teacher said she practiced with him over and over. She also showed him some breathing exercises he could do."

Benefits

- Improved mood
- Fewer disruptive behaviors
- Decreased anxiety and fear
- Improved communication
- Enhanced interpersonal interactions

"It is not a punishment room; it is not a time-out room—it is a room where you feel better going out than when you went in."

–Principal
El Dorado Elementary School
San Francisco, CA

SENSORY ROOMS

Sensory rooms are therapeutic spaces with a variety of equipment that provide students with personalized sensory input to meet their unique needs. Sensory rooms are not just for students with impairments, but for all students. Sensory-based activities are created for each child based upon their need to calm and focus themselves, become more engaged, and be prepared for learning and interacting with others. The plan for each child is called their "sensory diet".

A sensory room is not just a room filled with sensory equipment. There is a plan and purpose for every student with the equipment. For example, students are interviewed about their symptoms and reactions so the professional (might be an occupational therapist, behavior interventionist, student advocate, or educator) can understand if the student needs help calming or exciting their system. Behaviors also help the professional understand what the student needs most, but the ultimate goal is for the student to gain self-awareness so that they will be able to articulate their needs.

There are various categories of sensory input available: vestibular, proprioception, tactile, auditory, visual, or oral-motor. In some sensory rooms, there are color coded options for sensory input. According to each student's sensory diet, they can select a few activities from the specific colors or categories of sensory input to best meet their needs. Students engage in the activities prescribed and then check in with the professional to see if they are ready to return to their classroom. If they need more sensory input, they select another activity. In most cases, however, students are ready to return to the classroom after they have engaged in the activities specific to their individualized sensory diet.

Sensory rooms do not need expensive equipment to be beneficial. For example, a rocker or swing, weighted materials, a mini trampoline, and some tactile materials are enough to provide sensory input. The rooms, however, should have light covers or bubble tubes, since school lighting is often over-stimulating for students.

If a school does not have a room available, there are options to put rockers, weighted materials, and other sensory equipment in the classroom to offer support. Other schools create "brain trails" throughout their hallways, providing pictures on the walls or cues on the ground for students to engage in activities such as yoga moves, deep breathing, cross crawls, and wall pushes.

Time In Versus Time Out

When students show signs of dysregulation, they really need the help of caring adults to calm and quiet themselves. Dysregulation is a sign that a child can't regain control on their own. Common symptoms of emotional upset in children include hitting, crying, throwing, withdrawing, bullying, and oppositional behaviors. Adolescents may shut down in an effort to avoid their overwhelming feelings. In the classroom, you may notice students who are shut down in the forms of blank stares, withdrawal, falling asleep, daydreaming, or walking out of class. When a child acts out or shuts down, it is usually because they need to do something to regulate themselves and don't know how else to do it.

When students are emotionally upset or shut down, those are signs they are not able to resolve some dysregulation within themselves. They need adults to both help them identify the problem and to help them manage their response to it. In this context, the idea of "discipline" is not a useful or helpful place from which to begin. A more effective approach begins with two questions, "What does this child need?" and "How can I help meet this need?"

The first step in helping a child return to a calm or engaged state is supporting them both emotionally and based upon what their body needs. The most effective tool for reestablishing this is through connections. The "time in" approach encourages connection. This involves placing children physically near an adult for a period of time and providing calming words, empathetic non-verbal cues, and firm but caring boundaries.

HOW TO FACILITATE A "TIME IN"

- Invite the child to sit with you, take a walk with you, be near you (if very aggravated, don't touch).
- Acknowledge that the child is upset, mad, out of control, or just zoned out—let them know it is okay to have those feelings, but that it is not okay to hurt them self, others, or be disrespectful .
- Make eye contact, and be firm and kind.
- "I want to help you calm down" (adult must maintain a calm presence) or "I want to help you engage in class or with peers".
- Address misbehavior only after calm, but don't lecture—identify and note one or two strategies and then move on.
- Revisit the strategy again later when calm.
- Practice strategy.
- Most students need repetitive opportunities to practice new coping skills.

ACTIVITY:
Age-Specific Time In Approaches for Students

Based upon the time in concept, think of a few time in approaches you might implement for students of various ages.

- 5 years or younger (example: lap time)

_____

- 6-12 years (example: pull a chair close to you and ask the child to sit down)

_____

- 13-17 years (example: let's go for a walk together)

_____

Time Out vs. Time In	
TIME OUT	**TIME IN (CO-REGULATION)**
Kids act out because they WANT attention	Kids act out because they NEED attention
Time apart	Time together
Withdraw attention/disconnect	Give attention/connect
Very little opportunity to learn	Learning opportunity
Child is left to regain regulated state on their own	Adult is present to help child regain regulated state
Punitive, shame, rejection	Growth, empowerment, acceptance
Ineffective	Effective

Co-Regulation in Action

"Jayden, 5th grade, flipped over the desk when a classmate made a comment to him. He barged out of the room and sat on the table outside the classroom in the hall. The assistant principal was called, and she came and sat quietly next to him on the table and waited. After a few minutes they talked about what had happened and what he needed to do to fix it."

Jayden – Elementary School Social Worker

Time in provides CO-REGULATION — can be done with adult or with a peer.

"Samantha, 4th grade, came in late on the first day of the MEAP test. It was January and she had a fleece blanket wrapped around her. I greeted her and asked if she wanted the "MEAP snack" I was passing out. She cringed at the mention of the MEAP and crawled under her desk, wrapping the blanket around her so she was completely out of sight. Knowing the history of domestic violence in her family, I surmised she'd had a tough night or morning. I sat down next to her and asked if she was okay. She said yes, but stayed under the blanket. I asked if there was anything she needed while patting her back and she said no, she was okay, and she didn't need to talk to anyone. After I passed out the test, she slowly grabbed hers from the top of her desk and proceeded to complete it lying on the floor, wrapped in her blanket. The whole class watched quietly as I occasionally checked on her. During breaks, other students gathered around her, making sure she was okay. I made sure the social worker knew what was happening so she could follow up with the mom."

Samantha – 4th grade teacher

"Trevon, 4th grade, struggled in reading due to his inability to focus long enough to complete a sentence. One day we decided to try rubbing his back while he read. I sat next to him and gently rubbed the top of his back/shoulders. He sat still and read without stopping! Since then, I tried this with a lot of students and it worked with quite a few."

Trevon - District Occupational Therapist

"Skylar, 4th grade, despised writing and wouldn't write more than a word or two. After trying many of the usual strategies (drawing the story first, telling the story orally, making a timeline, scribing the beginning for him, etc.), I gave him a CD player with headphones playing popular songs. Skylar sat with his writers notebook, at his desk, and wrote FOUR pages! From then on, Skylar listened to music while he read and wrote."

Skylar – 4th grade student teacher

"Kayden, 5th grade, was always one of the last students into science class. His body was tense and his eyes darted around the room as he listened for any negative comments his peers were making about "him". We noticed that he seemed particularly calm when paired with Rylie, a quiet girl who loved to draw. When he was paired with her for the science investigations, he drew with her anytime they had a chance. We asked Kayden if he would like to sit next to Rylie during class and he said yes. We encouraged them to draw at the start of class. Kayden really seemed to feel safe around Rylie and mirrored her calm."

Kayden – 5th grade science teacher

> "Every child will be good if given an opportunity in an environment of love and activity."

Remember this...

STEP 4 HIGHLIGHTS

- You can't teach or practice emotional regulation or coping skills before emotional awareness.
- Taking time for social and emotional skill-building will be a benefit to you and your students.
- Time in – not time out.

STEP 5

Establish Safety

TRAUMA	SAFETY
HOPELESSNESS	HOPEFUL
POWERLESS	EMPOWERED
NO CONTROL	CHOICE
STUCK	SECURITY
CHAOS	CONSISTENCY

Many children in the United States do not grow up in homes that are fully protective, or in supportive neighborhoods. Their only felt sense of safety is at school. This experience of school safety, like school connectedness and belonging, is another significant protective factor.

Promoting a sense of physical and psychological safety throughout a school system, including how safety is defined by students, is one of the Substance Abuse and Mental Health Services Administration's (SAMHSA) key principles of a trauma-informed approach.

- **Physical Safety:** Your body is not in danger. If a threat presents itself, you are appropriately reactive to any warning signals to ensure your body is protected. You either remove yourself from the situation or defend yourself (fight or flight).

- **Emotional Safety:** You can identify your feelings in a situation, recognize what your intuition tells you, and act on these feelings appropriately.
- **Mental Safety:** You are able to access belief systems and patterns of thinking and awareness to accomplish what you want or need on a consistent basis.

Restoration of a sense of safety must be the immediate focus, and is essential for helping traumatized children heal. At the core of trauma is the overwhelming sense of powerlessness and absence of a sense of safety.

When you feel terror, you don't feel safe. Terror is the experience of feeling totally unsafe and powerless to do anything about our situation. Even if the trauma has passed, the experience of terror may still dominate.

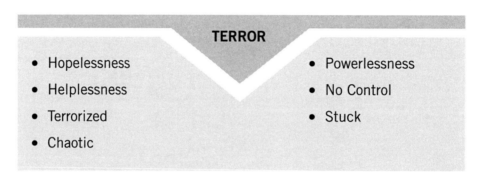

While feeling unsafe may be accompanied by violence, it doesn't have to be. The experience of safety includes these characteristics:

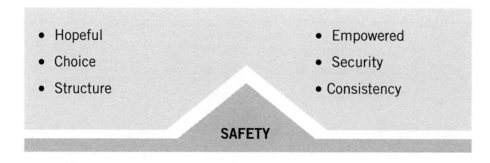

How can we help students experience these characteristics? If we think about the experience of stress and trauma as sensory experiences, it makes sense to think about safety in the same way.

ACTIVITY:
Safe Schools

Reflect upon the following questions. There are some ideas to get you started — add 5 examples to each.

- What would a safe school look like? Colors, artwork, windows, physical structure, adult's faces...

_____

- What would students hear in school to experience safety? Music, voice levels, bells, encouraging words...

_____

- What about a smell — what would a safe school smell like? Clean, airy, the outdoors...

_____

- How would a student's body feel in a safe school? Calm, relaxed muscles, confident posture, steady breathing...

_____

- What about taste? Is there a taste associated with a safe school? Fresh food, access to snacks if needed, clean and safe drinking water...

_____

Research demonstrates that academic achievement improves in schools where students feel physically and emotionally safe, and where school cultures support reasonable rules that are carefully explained and fairly enforced. A healthy learning community that is physically, emotionally, and intellectually safe is the foundation for a comprehensive high-quality education.

Children need age-appropriate knowledge about what adults are doing to help create safe and secure environments. For the greatest impact, this should not be vague assurances but specific, tangible ways that safety is being created. This may involve sharing simple facts such as, "anyone who wants to enter our school building has to check in at the office." Taking this a step further, an educator can walk the child through the process of what happens when an adult enters the school; they are buzzed in, they have to show their identification, etc. This helps to reinforce connection and safety.

FEELING SAFE IS KNOWING:

- What I say will be heard, not laughed at.
- What I draw will be enjoyed, not called weird.
- When I make a mistake, someone will help, not call me stupid.
- Nobody will tease me.
- Nobody will bully me.
- I will have someone to sit with.
- I will have someone to play with.
- I will have someone to talk to.
- I know my schedule.
- My teacher will be even tempered.

ACTIVITY:
Voice and Choice

Empower students by allowing them to make choices. Select one or two examples from the following list and expand upon it in the space provided.

- [ ] Allow students to have ownership over class routines.
- [ ] Provide choices in how students learn. Provide a variety of learning options (writing, drawing, creating, making, showing, speaking).

- [ ] Use student surveys to find out what's working and what isn't working – what do students like and what do they not like.
- [ ] Class meetings can improve communication among students and allow for modeling, sharing, problem solving, and celebrating success.
- [ ] Use a variety of lesson structures. Students should have an opportunity to learn no matter their preferred learning style.

- How can you implement one of these ideas in your classroom or school?

_____

_____

_____

_____

_____

_____

SCHEDULE/ROUTINE

CASE EXAMPLE: JAMAL

Jamal arrived late to school on most mornings. As he hurried to his locker and then to his seat in the classroom, he often blurted out to the teacher, "What is the plan for today?" The teacher, already involved in the morning lesson would respond, "Jamal, please take your seat" or "Jamal, we've already gone through that this morning." Jamal was polite and always took his seat but he was never quite settled. He fumbled with papers and looked around the classroom and almost never focused on what was being taught. Jamal's teacher attended a Trauma-Informed Schools training and decided to try a new approach. The next day Jamal was late to school. He entered the class and like always asked, "What is the plan for today?" Jamal's teacher patiently stopped the current lesson and responded, "Jamal, I am so glad you are here, today I started with a morning meeting and our math lesson, but I haven't had a chance to tell the class the rest of our plan for the day. Let's do that now." The teacher proceeded to outline the day's schedule both verbally and in written form on the white board. Then, he asked the class, "Any questions?" Jamal raised his hand and said, "My only question is can we go over our plan every day at this time?"

- Have a daily schedule posted each morning.
- Walk kids into "specials" and join in the beginning of class (e.g., run the lap around the gym for warm up, sit next to them for the beginning of art, help them get their computer started, etc.).
- Prepare, prepare, prepare: Show students the website for the museum you're going to visit, explain what is going to happen at field day and practice the events, walk through everything you can – don't just talk about it.
- Assemblies are really hard for many students. A gym full of closely packed, loud kids

would make anyone stressed. Practice how to walk into the gym, up the stairs, etc., BE-FORE the assembly. Tell the students what the assembly is for, and who will be there. Sit next to kids who needed some extra security, and have headphones for those sensitive to the noise.

- If school rules exist such as: "If a students forgets their lunch card, they have to go to the end of the line", always make sure kids have their cards when lining up for lunch. Set your students up for success with all school rules.

Some specific routines put in place for individual kids:

> Mauria, 1st grade, was always late to class from breakfast. She argued and was aggressive with other students in the cafeteria. We asked a 5th grader if she would want to sit with her during breakfast and then walk her to class, which was down another wing of the building. Every morning the 5th grader did this. They developed a relationship, and Mauria started her day on a positive note.

> Casey, a kindergarten student, ran around the cafeteria, grabbing kids' food. When his teacher picked him up, he ran down the hall and into the classroom. We asked him if he would want to eat lunch with Mike, the behavior specialist, and he loved it. Mike walked him to class afterwards. This really helped him calm down.

Trauma-informed resilient schools understand that students do better when they know what to expect. Children who have experienced trauma are always wondering:

- What is going to happen next?
- Is something bad going to happen?
- What are they going to do or say?
- Will I be able to control my emotions?
- Will I be able to control my behavior?

- Who will be there?
- Who will I sit with?
- Will they like me?
- Will the teacher think my answer is good?
- What if I can't learn how to do the problem before the test?

Schedules are the key to creating an "I know what I can expect next" school and classroom climate. Students learn and behave better when there is a routine in place. If the schedule is consistent, students pick up patterns very quickly. Once a pattern is set, students can infer, for instance, that lunch comes after math time. This way, there aren't too many unknowns. This understanding gives the student a sense of control.

Schedules help build trust between students and educators. Predictability makes students feel safe and that the adult in charge cares about meeting their needs. When students have too many unknowns, anxiety builds up and they start showing emotional and behavioral dysregulation as a result of the inconsistency. For example, on days when there are school assemblies, schedules often get changed. Let's say that a student is used to having lunch at 11:30 am every day, but on the assembly day the class will eat later – around 12:45 pm. You may see the student acting out or not enjoying the things that they normally do. Breaking a schedule can throw a child completely off, especially those with trauma histories.

However, some flexibility is important. For example, if your schedule says your music time goes for 30 minutes and you're done in only 10 minutes because the children are telling you they are finished, then move on to the next activity on your schedule. Students who have experienced trauma may need to see visual schedules in the classroom or on their desks. They may also benefit from frequent reminders of what is coming next during the school day.

Kids who have been through trauma worry about what is going to happen next. A daily routine in the classroom can be calming, so try to provide structure and predictability whenever possible. Since words may not sink in for traumatized students, try sensory cues. Besides explaining how the day will unfold, have signs or storyboards that show each activity of the day — math, reading, lunch, recess.

Routines help create a sense of safety. Turning routines into rituals add meaning and interaction.

COMMON FEARS
OF SCHOOL-AGED CHILDREN

1. Parent death

2. Parent divorce

3. Storms and natural disasters

4. Being alone (at home,
    at school in the hallway)

5. Fear of a teacher who is angry

6. Scary news, TV shows, movies

7. Injury/illness
    (going to doctor/hospital)

8. Dying

9. Rejection

10. Failure

ACTIVITY:
Turning Routines into Rituals

Write the ways you can turn your school routines or schedule into a ritual in the chart below.

Routine	How to Make It Into a Ritual
LINING UP	TEACHER: SPAGHETTI! (SIGNAL TO LINE UP) STUDENTS: MEATBALLS! (WHILE LINING UP)

ACTIVITY:
Feeling Vulnerable at School

Fill in the boxes below with other times students may feel unsafe or vulnerable during the school day. What are you doing to make them feel safe? Write specific things your school could do to help.

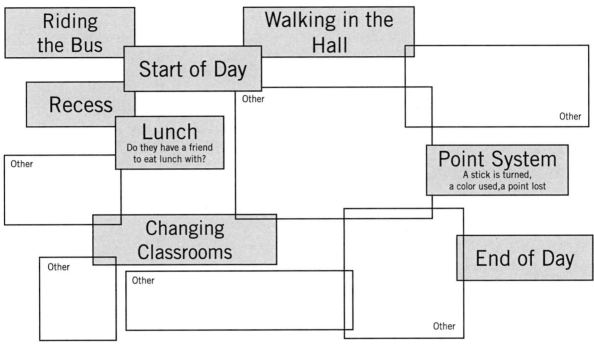

What are you doing today to make these times safer?

What are the things your school could do better?

ACTIVITY:
Circle of Safety

Use words or images to complete the circle of safety. Suggestions are listed on the next page.

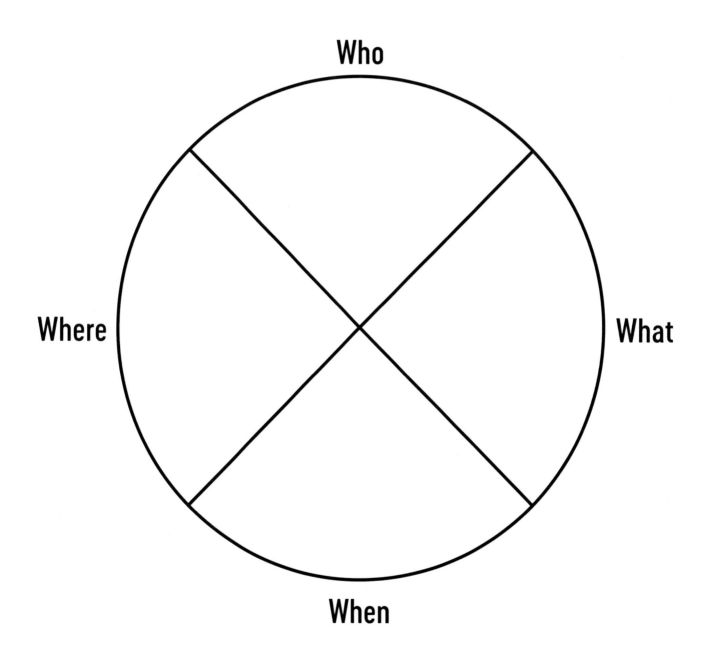

Circle of Safety continued

Circle or add from the lists below to your Circle of Safety Activity:

WHO	WHAT	WHEN	WHERE
MOM	SCHOOL WORK	MORNING	HOME - MOM
DAD	SPORTS	AFTER SCHOOL	HOME - DAD
GRANDMA	DANCE	AT SCHOOL	SCHOOL
GRANDPA	ART	IN THE BATHROOM	STORE
AUNT	WATCHING TV	BEDTIME	MALL
UNCLE	READING	OTHER	PLAYGROUND
COUSIN	INTERNET		GRANDMA'S
NEIGHBOR	PARTIES		GRANDPA'S
TEACHER	DRIVING		CHURCH
PRINCIPAL	OTHER		OTHER
FRIEND			
BUS DRIVER			
COACH			
PASTOR/PRIEST			
OTHER			

VIOLENCE SPECIFIC TO SCHOOL

Children and adolescents in urban environments experience higher rates of exposure to violence (Campbell & Schwartz, 2006).

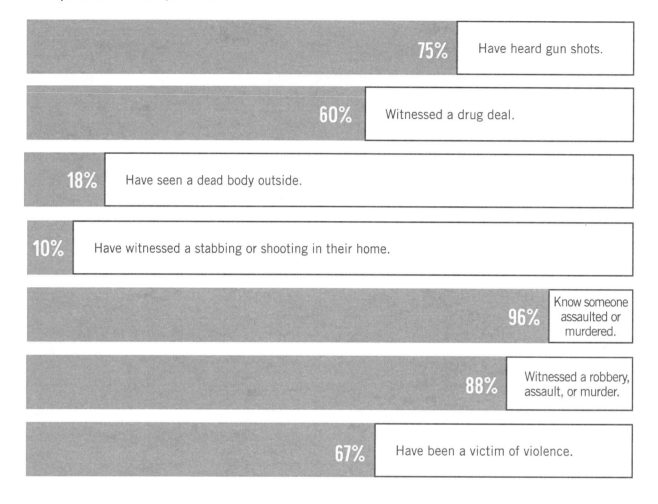

75%	Have heard gun shots.
60%	Witnessed a drug deal.
18%	Have seen a dead body outside.
10%	Have witnessed a stabbing or shooting in their home.
96%	Know someone assaulted or murdered.
88%	Witnessed a robbery, assault, or murder.
67%	Have been a victim of violence.

The National Center for Injury Prevention and Control considers school violence a public health problem. School violence is youth violence that occurs on school property, on the way to or from school, or during a school sponsored event. A young person can be a victim, a perpetrator, or a witness of school violence. School violence may also involve or impact adults. Youth violence includes various behaviors. Some violent acts – such as bullying, pushing, and shoving – can cause more emotional harm than physical harm. Other forms of violence, such as gang violence and assault (with or without a weapon), can lead to serious injury or death.

STATISTICS

While school-associated violent deaths are rare, non-fatal violent victimizations at school among students are not. Of all youth homicides, less than 2.6% occur at school, and this percentage has been relatively stable for the past decade. In 2014, there were about 486,000 non-fatal violent victimizations at school among students 12 to 18 years of age (Zhang et al, 2015).

Approximately 9% of teachers report they have been threatened with injury by a student from their school; 5% of school teachers report they have been physically attacked by a student from their school.

In 2013, 12% of all students ages 12 to 18 reported that gangs were present at their school during the school year.

In a 2015 nationally representative sample (Zhang et al.) of youth in grades 9-12:

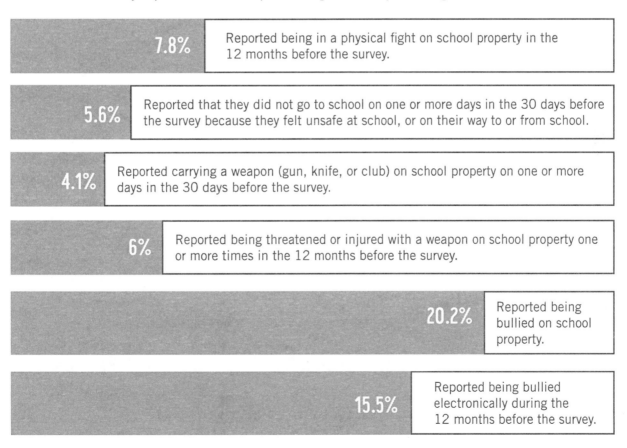

7.8%	Reported being in a physical fight on school property in the 12 months before the survey.
5.6%	Reported that they did not go to school on one or more days in the 30 days before the survey because they felt unsafe at school, or on their way to or from school.
4.1%	Reported carrying a weapon (gun, knife, or club) on school property on one or more days in the 30 days before the survey.
6%	Reported being threatened or injured with a weapon on school property one or more times in the 12 months before the survey.
20.2%	Reported being bullied on school property.
15.5%	Reported being bullied electronically during the 12 months before the survey.

Q How can I make school a safe place when I teach in one of the most dangerous cities in the entire country? It seems like there's not a week that goes by when the students aren't telling me about a stabbing or a drive by shooting. How do I help my students cope with the ongoing news of student deaths as the result of violence and gang activity?

It's so tough for caring teachers to know they can't control what's happening to their students outside of the classroom. The best thing you can do is put a routine in place that allows for meaningful interactions and connection with students. You may hear students say things like, "What is the point" or "Why should we try, we could die tomorrow." Educators can engage students in activities that provide them with a sense of hope — even if it is just talking about activities in the near future they are looking forward to doing. Allow for movement and physical activity breaks in the classroom so they can experience some fun. Encourage students to seek out safe places. You can become an advocate for after school programs, clubs, and playground equipment.

HAVE YOU CONSIDERED MINORITY STRESS?

Violence, abuse, neglect, poverty, death, substance abuse, etc. can be trauma-inducing experiences. But can the color of your skin? How about your sexuality or gender identity? Research says yes. Being a member of a non-dominant group in the United States, particularly African-American, Latino, or a member of the LGBT community produces something called minority stress — increased levels of stress attributed to living with systemic racism, prejudice, homophobia, transphobia, and implicit bias on a daily basis for one's entire life. Much like adverse childhood experiences, this stress can lead to negative health and well-being outcomes later in life like diabetes, heart disease, depression, substance abuse, etc. Knowing this, trauma-informed resilient schools must act to make their learning environments safe and inclusive spaces for these young people. With Starr Commonwealth, educators can receive training and coaching on doing just that - becoming allies to students who need them.

Remember this...

STEP 5 HIGHLIGHTS

- It is not what the students know about feeling safe, it is about what they experience as safe.
- Routines create consistency and predictability.
- Identify who, what, when, and where students feel vulnerable, and put a plan in place to offer them a safe experience.

STEP 6

Promote Play and Breaks

Recess is defined by the Center for Disease Control and Prevention (CDC) as regularly scheduled periods within the school day for unstructured physical activity and play that serve as a necessary break from instructional time in the classroom. All too often, schools are taking away recess to accommodate additional time for academic subjects, or are withdrawing recess for punitive or behavioral reasons. Trauma-informed resilient schools recognize recess as a time for rest, imagination, movement, and socialization. After play, recess, or breaks, students of all ages are more attentive and better able to perform cognitively. It doesn't matter if recess is performed indoors or outdoors; when implemented, students are more attentive and productive. Even if students spend their time socializing, the break from instruction time is a benefit (Ramstetter et al, 2011).

REVOKING RECESS

The word punishment is derived from the Latin word for penalty, poena, and literally means "to inflict suffering." Typically, in learning environments, punishment means "to inflict pain in order to control or correct behavior." This helps one to understand why educators so often use revocation of recess as their "go to" punishment. When working with elementary-aged children, it is assumed that recess is their favorite or most pleasurable time of the school day, so to take it away is to inflict the most pain (or suffering) possible, thereby making the student afraid of committing the infraction again so as not to lose their recess again. Though controlling people through fear of punishment can work to some degree (as long as the threat of punishment exists), it does little to nothing to teach individuals how to behave properly, and is detrimental to positive relationship building between the authority figure and the person affected. For example, imagine if teachers were punished for not turning in lesson plans on time by revoking their vacation time. It may prompt some teachers to turn in their plans in a timelier fashion, but what would it do to their sense of job satisfaction, appreciation, and relationship with their administrator? Would they have a better understanding of the value behind turning in well-constructed lesson plans in a timely manner? Would they work hard to write better lesson plans? Would they stay at the school long-term? It is also important to consider that punishment for punishment's sake can spiral out of control. What does the teacher do when he or she faces a misbehaving student who does not particularly care for recess? Believe it or not, there are teachers who have responded by revoking other cherished things instead: library time, snack, gym, art, etc. In one's pursuit for the perfect way to "inflict suffering", the very purpose of school can be undermined.

Recess also promotes an emotional regulation opportunity for students to foster connections by providing them with an opportunity to engage in peer interactions. Activity helps to improve the school climate by allowing students time to develop communication skills like negotiation, cooperation, sharing, problem solving, perseverance, and self-control (Robert Wood Johnson Foundation, 2011).

Play breaks of 15 minutes or more result in:

- Better teacher ratings of classroom behavior
- Increased attentiveness in class
- Increased productivity
- Improved ability to store new information
- Increased cognitive capacity

In some schools, students are lacking access to recess and breaks because of reduced school resources like physical education, art, music, parks, and playgrounds. Other schools are under tremendous pressure to increase academic achievement, and often increase instruction time while decreasing time spent with play and activities. The American Academy of Pediatrics agrees that schools should ban games and activities that are not safe, but that they should never discontinue recess. If a school is concerned about safety, there is a resource that can be found in the resources section of this book that discusses safety of playground equipment and meets federal guidelines. Some schools in areas with a high risk of violence may require additional protective measures to ensure the safety of children (American Academy of Pediatrics, 2013).

Tell the class that you are scheduling regular recess and brain breaks throughout the day. Let them know that you will allow them to play, have free time, and stretch. If you build in breaks and movement before behavior gets dysregulated, you are setting students up to succeed. A child may be better able to make it through a 20-minute block of work if they can anticipate a break will follow to help recharge them for the next task.

DURATION OF RECESS AND BREAKS

National guidelines support the need for regularly scheduled recess. However, the length of the recess period has not been established. Most schools have recess duration ranges from 20-60 minutes per day, but this varies widely from school to school. In countries outside of the United States, recess and breaks are longer. For example, in Japan, primary school-aged children have a

10-15 minute break every hour of the school day for a total of 90 minutes of recess or breaks per day. This is based upon research indicating attention spans begin to wane after 40 to 50 minutes of instruction time. Minimizing or eliminating recess is counterproductive to achievement, as a growing body of evidence suggests that recess promotes not only physical health and social development, but also cognitive performance. On the basis of abundant scientific studies, withholding recess for punitive or academic reasons would seem to go against intended student outcomes such as cognitive, social, and emotional development and might have unintended, negative consequences (Stevenson & Lee, 1990; American Academy of Pediatrics, 2013).

A survey of nearly 2,000 educators indicated 78 percent think students who spend regular time in unstructured outdoor play have better concentration and problem-solving capabilities, and are more creative than students who do not. Many studies confirm that access to nature in schools has a positive impact on student focus and learning by improving attentiveness, test scores, and performance. Whenever possible, it is recommended that school lessons and assignments either be conducted outside or sandwiched in between breaks where children have time to play and enjoy nature (National Wildlife Association, 2010).

The American Academy of Pediatrics indicates that play protects children's emotional development in comparison to a loss of free time, which can be a source of stress, anxiety, and even depression for some kids. Researchers have also found kids who play together and organize games on their own experience less social isolation. Children who spend too much time indoors watching television or playing video games can become isolated or withdrawn, even if they think they are connecting online. The Center for Disease Control (CDC) recommends at least one hour per day of physical activity for kids.

When teachers and parents say to a child, "Stop staring out the window and pay attention to your school work," perhaps they should consider the child's gesture as a cue that play is needed.

"Recess serves as a necessary break from the rigors of concentrated, academic challenges in the classroom. But equally important is the fact that safe and well-supervised recess offers cognitive, social, emotional, and physical benefits that may not be fully appreciated with a decision is made to diminish it. Recess is unique from, and a complement to, physical education – not a substitute for it. The American Academy of Pediatrics believes that recess is a crucial and necessary component of a child's development and, as such, it should not be withheld for punitive or academic reasons."

– (*American Academy of Pediatrics, 2013*) For the full paper on the Crucial Role of Recess in School go to http://pediatrics.aapublications.org/content/131/1/183

TEAM BUILDING ACTIVITIES

Recognize the need for recess and breaks from instruction to allow students time for rest, imagination, movement, and socialization. Adding team building activities each week (which ties in with PBIS by recognizing hard work through celebrating), like a "Fun Friday," is a great way for students to shine in areas other than academics. There are many team building activities on line to access filled with ideas. (https://www.teampedia.net/wiki/index.php/Main_Page)

As a grade level, have each teacher be in charge of planning the team building activity for the week. Keep a "team building" journal where students can write about their experience.

- How did they feel during the activity?
- What were the sensations before, during, and after?
- Highlight the behaviors needed to be a team player. What behaviors/actions did they notice in their teammates that helped the team meet their goal? (This is where you can highlight listening, problem solving, and generosity skills).

Adding team building activities is a great way to add play and movement to student schedules. They will also help you implement some of the concepts you learned about focusing on resilience, fostering connections, and practicing social and emotional skill development.

Team building activities are activities done for fun – no content required. Team building activities strengthen the relationship between groups of students (a class!) and help students communicate more effectively with one another. Activities can be as quick as less than ten minutes, or as long as a whole class period. Here are some ideas to get you started:

Hula Hoop Hop

Students hold hands to form a circle. Place a hula hoop between one set of students. Students then work together to get the hoop all the way around the circle, holding hands the entire time.

Tic-Tac-Toe

Human tic-tac-toe is super easy, and super-fast. Use tape (or paper) to lay out a tic-tac-toe board on the ground. Divide students into two groups – Xs and Os. Groups switch off sending a student to the board. Once a team has won the game, or once the game is tied, the game begins again. To show which team they are on, students make an "X" or "O" with their arms.

Rope Shapes

Bring a long rope to class. Have each student grab a section of the rope. Then, instruct students to create various shapes with the rope. Squares, rectangles, triangles, pentagons, etc. This activity is a great way to give students practice being group leaders. For each shape you can assign two or three students to be the group leaders, while the other students must quietly follow directions. Group leaders instruct students on where they should move to help form the shape. This activity can also be done with two groups of students and two pieces of rope.

Plastic Cup Tower

Divide students into groups of five or six. Give each group a stack of plastic cups. See which group can build the tallest tower in a certain amount of time (two to three minutes is really fun!) This activity can be done in less than 10 minutes, or you can play once, then have students switch groups and do it multiple times.

No Talking Line Up

Divide students into two groups. Then, have each group form a line without talking. One of my favorite lines to have students form is one where students sort themselves by birthday. Another way is to have them sort themselves alphabetically. Alphabetically is fun at the beginning of the year when students are still learning each other's names. They can use hand signs to show letters or numbers, but no words. First group to form a line wins!

Balloon Toss

Divide students into two groups. Each group should form a circle. Have each student bring two pencils (or pens) to the activity. Give each group a balloon. Have each group blow up the balloon. Then, have students pass the balloon around their group using only the pencils.

ACTIVITY:
Team Building

Jot down some of your own ideas for activities to help facilitate team building that you can try in your classroom.

_____

_____

_____

_____

_____

_____

_____

BRAIN BREAKS

If you haven't heard of brain breaks, they are short mental breaks (which include physical activity) that normally last less than five minutes, and are used to refocus and wake up your students. A few ideas to use are listed below.

Dance Break

Put on some music, turn off the lights, and DANCE! These websites provide great access to brain break music and activities:

- https://www.youtube.com/user/TheLearningStation
- http://blog.reallygoodstuff.com/67-kid-friendly-brain-break-songs-and-musicians-for-the-classroom/
- https://howywood.com/brain-breaks/fun-kids-songs-brain-breaks/

Social Time

This game allows students to do the one thing they always want to do: talk! Set the timer for one minute and let the students mingle with a partner. When the timer goes off, everyone has to find a new partner to mingle with, and so on, for as many times as you think is necessary.

Simon Says

You can be Simon, or switch it up and let one of the students. Students are not quite sure how to play "Simon Says", so you may need a refresher course for the kids.

Brain trails are brain breaks located in school hallways. In one middle school, the school social worker and occupational therapist worked together to create a brain trail system. Students would log in in the media center on a computer or tablet set up in hallways. When logging in, they indicate how they are feeling (tired, wound up, angry, etc.). The tablets then direct them to activities specific to supporting their identified feeling. The student engages in the activity, and then logs out indicating how they feel after the activity is completed. This provides data to the school's behavior specialists and occupational therapists. Then, there are follow-up meetings scheduled with each student who uses the brain trails where the student has an opportunity to learn similar sensory or regulatory input strategies that can be used in the classroom.

Additional practical ways to add play into classrooms to support learning and self-regulation:

Find someone in the class who...
- Loves peanut butter
- Hates marshmallows
- Is double jointed
- Can touch the tip of their nose with their tongue
- Has visited more than 3 different countries

Real or Fake? Do a Google search for weird fun facts!
- Elephants can understand sign language – real or fake?
- Clouds weigh over a ton – real or fake?

Have students line up in order of...
- Height
- Birth month
- Shoe size
- Middle name alphabetical order

ACTIVITY:
As Easy as ABC

Spell your first name and connect a stretch or movement with each letter:

ABC MOVEMENT WORD IDEAS:

Arching	Fishing	Kick-boxing	Praying	Uplifting
Bending	Golfing	Lunging	Quivering	Violin playing
Climbing	Hugging	Motoring	Running	Walking
Dancing	Ice skating	Nodding	Swimming	eXercising
Energizing	Jumping	Opening	Twirling	Yodeling
				Ziplining

Here is an example for the name Julie:

J - JUGGLING
U - UNDERWATER SWIMMING
L - LAUGHING
I - ICE SKATING
E - EASTER EGG HUNTING

MORE PLAY AS A CONSEQUENCE

In one trauma-informed school, a teacher decided not to take away recess for behavior problems in the classroom. Instead, she informed the student that she wanted them to spend the first half of their recess playing a game with her! (Time in.) She used this time as an opportunity to not only connect, but teach the student some coping skills, social skills, or relationship building techniques while playing. Brilliant!

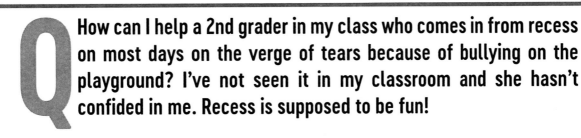

Q How can I help a 2nd grader in my class who comes in from recess on most days on the verge of tears because of bullying on the playground? I've not seen it in my classroom and she hasn't confided in me. Recess is supposed to be fun!

Ask the student and others, such as the recess monitor, what is happening on the playground. Link the student to a peer buddy and an adult that she feels safe going to, or giving a signal to when she is not having a good day. The code can be a wink or a silly word that alerts the adult she needs support. Bullying might not be violent; it can come in the form of a look or even a whisper. While it might not seem traumatic to adults, peers are the center of students' lives, and if they aren't accepting of them, that's traumatic. Intervene before the situation spirals into something that's out of control.

Bring playfulness to students of all ages while they learn

- Individual and group experiences
- Invent, design, build
- Gym
- Make believe/imaginative writing
- Science experiments
- Free choice: student directed learning
- Playground
- Art
- Problem solving

ACTIVITY:
Recess Reflection

What is the recess policy at your school? What about breaks during instruction time? How might you be able to incorporate more play into students' school day?

_____

_____

_____

_____

_____

ACTIVITY:
Create a Brain Break Calendar

Use the calendar template on the next page and write at least one brain break for every day on the calendar.

Ideas to include:
- Give your class a riddle or tell a joke
- Play Simon Says
- Doodle for 5 minutes
- Do 25 jumping jacks
- Play Rock Paper Scissors
- Dance to a top 40 hit

Brain Break Calendar

SUN	MON	TUE	WED	THU	FRI	SAT

Remember this...

STEP 6 HIGHLIGHTS

- Children need the freedom and time to PLAY. Play is not a luxury. Play is a NECESSITY!
- Breaks from instruction time help improve behavior and academic achievement.

STEP 7

Believe the Link Between Private Logic and Behavior

What matters most when working with at-risk and traumatized youth are not the symptoms of trauma, but the experience of trauma. Specifically, it's how that trauma impacts students and the way they see themselves, as well as how they interact with others. There is a distinct link between a student's private logic and their behavior. Private logic can be described as how a person views themselves, others, and the world around them. Private logic is created as a result of experiences. Based on that logic, they act accordingly. Think of private logic as an invisible backpack. In the backpack, a student carries around beliefs about themselves, beliefs about the adults that take care of them, and lastly, beliefs about other people they interact with in their lives and beliefs about the world. This logic is a result of experiences – both good and bad – over the course of development and life. If their lives have been filled with fear, abandonment, and anger, their private logic will be consistent with those experiences. They will view themselves as scared and powerless, others will not be trusted, and the world to them is seen as a scary place. If their lives have been filled with comfort, connection, and love, their logic will be consistent with those experiences. They will view themselves as capable and valued. They will see others as consistent and approachable, and will view the world as filled with opportunities of goodness and hope.

Traumatized children's behavior can be perplexing, unpredictable, and demanding. Sometimes, children of trauma do things to make others reject them. Unconsciously, based upon their private logic, they try to prove to themselves and others that the low self-image they have of themselves and others is indeed true. As mentioned above, depending upon their early childhood experiences, a student may view themselves and others in a variety of ways – confident or lacking self-worth, trusting or distrustful of others, comfortable asking for help or afraid of rejection.

Trauma can also impact the way children interact with peers and educators. Children who have experienced trauma have difficulty reading others – they can be distrustful and suspicious of anyone who tries to make a connection with them, especially if that is not consistent with previous experiences. Research indicates that children who have been exposed to violence often have difficulty responding to social cues, and may withdraw from social situations or even bully others because they want to portray themselves as powerful, but inside they feel helpless and hopeless. For example, children who have experienced physical abuse are less likely to engage in meaningful relationships. In addition, they tend to be more aggressive and negative when they interact with others. Students who have experienced trauma may also feel like adults have failed to keep them safe, and therefore may be distrustful of school professionals – or they interpret rules and consequences as punishment rather than as safety measures and opportunities to learn.

PRIVATE LOGIC IN THE CLASSROOM

Imagine an eleven-year-old student who, their entire life, has experienced that when adults in their home yell, someone gets hit or hurt. And then this student is in your classroom and you, in a well-intentioned and benign manner, raise your voice to get the attention of the class. When this happens, he is immediately triggered based on his past experiences. And then his best friend sitting next to him pokes him in the shoulder. The student reacts, possibly hitting his best friend. On the surface this looks like an irrational, unstable, and aggressive behavior. But underneath, based on the student's private logic, there is some level of rationality to what has occurred, but his body is still scared. We have to be curious rather than certain when observing behavior that seems to not make sense on the outside.

 **How can I help my first grade student whose family is going through a really difficult divorce? I am seeing regression in my student and a lot of anxiety around pickup and drop-off, and I want to approach her parents in a useful and non-confrontational way.**

Divorce is tough on students when they're at home and at school, and your student is lucky to have a teacher who recognizes that and wants to help. Let the parents know you are noticing changes. Don't bring up the divorce. Focus on the child and what you are seeing in class.

If they tell you about the divorce, you are in the know, but don't speculate. This will make the parent feel defensive and view you as placing blame rather than trying to help. Instead, ask them what behavior they're seeing at home. Ask if there is anything you can do.

The child will benefit most from consistency and routine in the classroom. Try to give your student ways to calm down on a sensory level—like breathing or stretching—to work through anxiety she may be feeling from home.

While it may be frustrating that you can't control what happens when your student leaves your classroom, you can feel good about the fact that the strategies you teach your student to use at school can translate to help her deal with the stress she experiences at home too.

ACTIVITY:
Exploring Private Logic

Read the statement and then answer the questions. What behaviors might you see as a result?

I will do whatever I have to do to let you know that I am terrified.

- How might this student view themself?

_____

- How might this student view others?

_____

- How might this student view the world?

_____

I think I want to run for student council.

- How might this student view themself?

_____

- How might this student view others?

_____

- How might this student view the world?

_____

I will do whatever I need to do in order to control you and your responses – I don't trust you and I need to survive.

- How might this student view them self?

_____

- How might this student view others?

_____

- How might this student view the world?

_____

I can't wait to see how I did on my English homework.

- How might this student view themself?

_____

- How might this student view others?

_____

- How might this student view the world?

_____

I will fight any experience, any activity, any person that tries to assert power over me – I don't want to feel any more out of control that I already do.

- How might this student view themself?

_____

- How might this student view others?

_____

- How might this student view the world?

_____

My friend is home sick but I am sure there is another person who will eat lunch with me.

- How might this student view themself?

_____

- How might this student view others?

_____

- How might this student view the world?

_____

I will not do what you want me to do because, if I fail, you will laugh at me and reject me.

- How might this student view themself?

_____

- How might this student view others?

_____

- How might this student view the world?

_____

If my mom has to work during my vocal concert, I will just ask my aunt if she can come to watch.

- How does this student view themself?

_____

- How does this student view others?

_____

- How does this student view the world?

_____

Behavior should be viewed as a clue – it is the student's way of communicating when they don't have the words to describe their experience. We learned in Step 2 that students are unlikely – and many times simply not capable – to use language, logic, or reason when they are experiencing toxic stress and trauma reactions. It is important to mention that behavior in the present may appear to be completely unrelated to what is happening in the here and now. However, because bodies remember stress and trauma, the behavior you see could be in response to a sensory reminder of something that occurred years ago. For example, if a student experienced being separated from a parent when they were younger and in a large crowd of people, their body may be triggered when attending a large school assembly. They might start to panic while in the crowd even if they are safe and their teacher is nearby.

ACTIVITY:
Private Logic Case Study

Directions: Think of a student you know and complete the following.

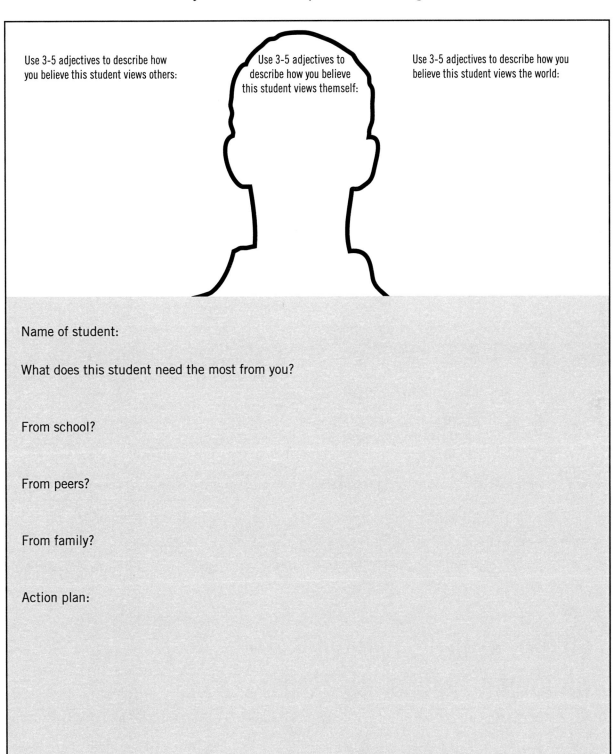

Use 3-5 adjectives to describe how you believe this student views others:

Use 3-5 adjectives to describe how you believe this student views themself:

Use 3-5 adjectives to describe how you believe this student views the world:

Name of student:

What does this student need the most from you?

From school?

From peers?

From family?

Action plan:

ACTIVITY:
Case Example: Ben

LOOKING AT BEN'S BEHAVIOR ONLY

Ben is a 5th grade boy. This morning when he arrived to school, the bell had already rung and he knew he was late. When Ben's teacher asked him for his homework, Ben told her he did not have it. Since this wasn't the first time he didn't have his homework, his teacher expressed frustration and took away his recess as a consequence. Later that morning, Ben's tablemate accidentally knocked his box of pencils onto the floor. As the other student was bending down to pick them up, Ben punched him in the stomach. His teacher began to yell at Ben to stop. Ben began to knock over chairs and swear at his teacher. Ben was brought to the principal's office and given a three-day suspension for fighting, disruptive behavior, and being disrespectful to his teacher.

BEN'S STORY

Ben is a 5th grade boy who has been living in a homeless shelter for the past three months. He and his mother left their home because Ben's father was physically abusive to both he and his mother. One night, Ben's father injured his mother so badly that they slept at a neighbor's home. The next day, Ben's mom told him that they weren't going to go home again, and they have been at the shelter since then. Last night the shelter was loud, so Ben barely slept. This morning, there was a long line for food, and after waiting over 45 minutes, he left the line and started to walk to school.

LOOKING AT BEN'S BEHAVIOR
THROUGH A TRAUMA-INFORMED LENS

This morning, when he arrived at school – late – his teacher asked him for his homework. When he didn't have it, she expressed frustration as this was not the first time he didn't have it, and took away his recess as a consequence. What Ben's teacher didn't know is that he was tired, hungry, and angry that he didn't have time to do his homework again. Later that morning, his tablemate accidentally bumped into him and knocked Ben's pencils off of his desk. Since Ben was already activated, Ben punched his classmate without thinking about it. His teacher, upset by Ben's outburst, began to yell at Ben to stop. The teacher's yelling further escalated Ben, so he began to scream and kick over chairs.

Ben was taken to the principal's office and given a three-day suspension for fighting and disruptive behavior. Ben therefore lost three days of instructional time and was left to spend more time in a noisy shelter. In addition, Ben's mom was not able to continue her job search because she had to supervise him at the shelter.

What are your reflections about Ben?

_____

_____

_____

_____

_____

_____

_____

_____

_____

RETHINKING "DISCIPLINE"

Out of school suspension is a commonly recognized method of exclusionary school discipline. It is generally recognized as the removal of a student from his or her daily routine for a temporary period of time. This could result in the student being removed from the school building altogether or being placed in a designated area, such as a school office or classroom, as a negative consequence for nearly any inappropriate behavior. Findings from the American Psychological Association's Zero Tolerance Task Force (2008) demonstrate little data to support any presumption of the effectiveness of out of school suspension for any reason (Baroni et al, 2016). Unfortunately, despite these findings, in any given year there are approximately 3.25 million students nationwide suspended across the United States. This figure has doubled in the past 40 years. Suspensions are even being used at the preschool level; 7,500 preschool students were suspended between 2011 and 2012, and 2,500 of those experienced multiple suspensions (U.S. Department of Education, Office for Civil Rights, 2014).

Students who are suspended are absent more than their peers, leading to academic deficiencies, feelings of alienation, inadequacy, and helplessness (Casella, 2003). The suspension experience becomes a magnification of how children of trauma often experience themselves and others – isolated and not worth the attention or time of the caring adults in their world. Exclusionary school tactics can result in shame, rejection, and the inability to bond with adults. In addition, suspension isn't effective at deterring poor student behavior (Baroni et al, 2016), yet many continue to implement suspension as a consequence. Trauma-informed schools encourage collaboration and mutual respect between administrators, educators, and students. Trauma-informed responses to challenging behavior, often driven from private logic, support the student rather than reprimand them.

Trauma-informed schools avoid consequences such as frequent detentions, suspensions, and time outs because they understand that behavior is driven by private logic and by past experiences. Instead, they use positive interactions and provide opportunities such as comfort corners, time ins, and restorative activities to support dysregulation. Exclusionary practices reinforce low self-worth, and encourage children to withdraw or engage in additional fight or flight behaviors. Practices that draw a student in and provide support to help the student regain control will calm down the survivor responses often activated when a child feels out of control or engaged in a power struggle with a school professional.

School disciplinary policies and procedures should be consistent, clearly communicated to both staff and students, and should strive to keep students in safe and supportive classrooms. In trauma-informed schools, behavior is addressed but is done with an awareness and sensitivity to childhood trauma that may be affecting such behavior (Cole et al, 2005; Wolpow et al, 2009). Alternatives to traditional school exclusionary disciplinary policies have the goal of increasing the amount of time students are in the classroom and learning. If a student needs to be removed from a classroom, it should be viewed as supportive, not punitive, and should provide a meaningful interaction with at least one adult and various intervention strategies to assist students in de-escalating and regulating their emotions so that they may return to the classroom as soon as they are ready.

Traumatized children are often taken out of the academic setting because of their frequent classroom disruptions. These are the same children who are at risk for dropping out of school altogether. Rather than sidelining them from school, they would benefit greatly from trauma-informed settings that can meet their unique challenges and needs induced by their trauma histories.

How do many adults respond to "opportunities" with challenging students?

1. Keep talking, I'm taking away recess minutes

This plays out in our schools almost every day. We design "consequences" that are intended to sting the student enough that they become fearful of breaking rules. It is a way of coercing students to behave the way we want them to rather than supporting them in ways to gain regulation and the ability to make decisions on their own. This is why Step 6 was dedicated to the importance of play. When you see an educator using this method, refer them to the American Academy of Pediatrics position paper about the crucial role of recess in our schools and the call to action to not take away recess as a consequence for academic or behavior challenges.

2. Law and Order

Many schools seem to be obsessed with "law and order", and use in-school suspension and detention systems. This communicates to students that they must "pay" for their offenses. Remember the core value, "Badness is not a normal condition but the result of misdirected energy and unmet needs"? We will come back to that core value as we move into re-thinking discipline. Let's look at the use of consequences, punishments, and rewards as a way to manage behavior in students.

3. The Disease Model

Would a doctor get mad at you if you came into their office sick – say, with an ear infection? Then came back the next week with another ear infection? Would they say, "When will you learn to stop getting ear infections?" No. The doctor would do everything to support and help you feel better. Adults often impose a different approach with behavior, and we see it as something the child can control or change. Or, we see symptoms and reactions and label them as a mental health disorder, and therefore interventions focus on drugs and behavior control.

What about level systems and clip or color charts, tickets, token economies? Are they fair? What do they teach? What do they reinforce?

Trauma-informed, resilience-focused schools do NOT use behavior management systems. Why?

- They work really well – for children who don't need them in the first place.
- They are a trigger for the fight, flight, and freeze response for children who experience trauma and toxic stress.
- They develop negative core beliefs (not, "I am having a bad day" but, "I am bad.")
- They are shame based ("I am bad because I didn't get a sticker, I am not valuable.")
- They are isolating.
- The do not take into account the individualized supports needed by all children in a classroom.
- They do not address the underlying causes of behavior.

Many schools have adopted behavior management systems that involve using a color chart displayed publicly in classrooms. Students names (or numbers which all students know after one week) are attached to a color, using a clothes pin, clip, or card, starting on a specific color each day, and then moving up or down according to their compliance with the classroom rules. The rationale behind a model like this is that we can embarrass students by making them move their name or number down in front of their peers, making them scared of misbehaving again. The problem is that many educators who use this type of model do not see kids' behavior improving. The same students move up and the same move down consistently. So then, is this model effective at helping student behavior improve? No. What really happens with behavior management systems is the students who do well end up spending time with others that do well, and the students that don't do well spend time with those who do the same. Overall, it is not effective.

SHAME AND GUILT

Guilt is connected to an action, whereas shame is connected to one's identity. Therefore, guilt can be healthy – shame is not. It is appropriate for a student to feel guilty for doing something that hurt another person. Feeling this way can be a powerful restorative motivator for making amends. However, feeling shameful, or bad, as a human being is never healthy. Our interventions should never make as student feel like they are bad.

CONSEQUENCES, PUNISHMENTS, AND REWARDS

NATURAL CONSEQUENCES

Natural and logical consequences are encouraged, as natural consequences are the most effective for the educator and the student.

Events that occur naturally:
- A student does not do their work and they receive a bad grade.
- A student pushes someone down, and then that student doesn't want to play with them anymore.
- A student breaks a computer, so the class no longer has one.

If there is not a natural consequence, then there probably should not be a rule. For events that do not occur naturally, the educator should create them with the intent to help—not to hurt. It is best to develop them with the student. For example:

- What can you do to help _____ feel better now that you've pushed them down? Do you need to write an apology? Should we set up a time where we can meet with them together?
- What ideas do you have about how to get your work done? Could you stay after school, or come in early tomorrow morning?
- How can we get the computer repaired? Could you pick up the room every day to earn some money to get it fixed?

PUNISHMENTS

Punishments belong to an autocratic value system in which authority figures dominate and reward or punish their "inferiors". There is no place for punishment in a trauma-informed, resilience-focused school. Punishment does not produce lasting change, only submission, and often escalates oppositional and defiant behavior.

REWARDS

Rewards that are not social in nature can cause problems (e.g., candy, tickets, coins, and prizes).

The problems rewards systems cause include:
- Extinguishing intrinsic motivation
- Diminishing performance
- Crushing creativity
- Crowding out good behavior
- Encouraging cheating, short-cuts, and other unethical behavior
- Rewards become addictive
- Foster short-term rather than long-term thinking

INTRINSIC VERSUS EXTRINSIC MOTIVATION

Intrinsic motivation is doing something for the sake of personal satisfaction. The primary motivator is internal (i.e., you don't expect to get anything in return). You are intrinsically motivated when you do something simply because it makes you feel good, is personally challenging, and/or leads to a sense of accomplishment. Usually an intrinsic motivator will meet one or more universal needs – belonging, mastery, independence, and/or generosity. For example, a student may be intrinsically motivated to do group work because it meets their need for belonging. Or, they might read because it satisfies their curiosity about the world and brings them a sense of curiosity and independence. Intrinsic motivation is doing something "just because."

Extrinsic motivation is doing something to earn a reward or to avoid a punishment. The primary motivator is external (i.e., you expect to get something for completing a certain task, or you want to avoid a consequence for not doing something). For example, a student studies for a test because they want to earn a good grade. Or, they behave well because they don't want to lose their recess. Students choose behaviors not because they enjoy them or find them satisfying, but in order to get something in return or avoid an adverse outcome.

Research shows that children continue to work toward their personal goals when intrinsic motivation is high. Stickers, clips, and color cards rely on extrinsic motivation. "You do this (sit, listen, and don't yell out), and you get this (sticker, clip up, and green card)." In the short-term, these systems can be motivating, but over time they are no longer enough. Another criticism is that sometimes kids get hooked on the rewards that come with extrinsic motivation. The more children are provided rewards for activities that have natural reward, the more they will expect reward and be unable to set or achieve goals without that extrinsic motivation. We've all had students that demand to know "What are we doing this for?" or "What do we get if we complete this task?" If we provide the "why" for our students too frequently, we stand in the way of them becoming independent learners.

Does extrinsic motivation affect a student's self-esteem?

When children rely too much on external motivation, they learn to compare themselves to others, and may give too much weight to other people's opinions. Do I have as many stickers as Mary? Is my teacher happy with me because I did the assignment the right way? If students are always looking outside of themselves for validation, they will be unhappy and unproductive when that validation is not readily available, and their self-esteem can suffer.

Supporting Intrinsic Motivation

The word intrinsic means to come from inside, so it seems counterintuitive to imply that we can train a student to be intrinsically motivated. While we cannot change who a student is as an individual, we can create the optimum environment to encourage students to develop their own intrinsic motivation. You will see how each one of these recommendations helps to meet one or more of our students' universal needs in the classroom and school setting.

Know your students

Get to know your kids as individuals, and discover what they're interested in and how they learn best. Then, design your instruction around these motivating factors. Change up your instruction to keep kids engaged and interested. Provide a mix of independent, partner, and group work. Use technology. Incorporate art. Spend time with them – join them for lunch or at their specials. Keep your finger on the pulse of your students and adjust as necessary.

Give students ownership of their environment

Involve your students in creating the guiding principles of your classroom community. Work together to establish the optimal learning environment for that particular group of individuals. Like all humans, your students are more likely to take care of something they helped to create.

Make sure students have a solid foundation

Explicitly teach basic skills so that students have a solid foundation of knowledge to build upon. Intrinsic motivation will come from being able to tackle complex tasks. Build up students' confidence and make sure they have the resources they need before they begin.

Practice setting goals

Setting student goals improves both motivation and achievement, encourages a growth mindset, and also supports the development of skills students need to be prepared for their futures.

Give specific feedback

Give students feedback that focuses on their strengths instead of their weaknesses, and be as specific as you possibly can. Instead of saying "Great job!" or "You're so smart," tie your comments directly to the student's effort. For example, "Your essay turned out so well because you created an excellent outline to work from," or "Your conclusion from the science lab was so insightful because you made very keen observations."

Tap into students' innate curiosity

Encourage students to take on assignments simply because they want to know more, instead of feeling required to do so just to receive a grade.

As much as possible, allow students choice in their work

When students are given choices, they perceive classroom activities as more important. This increases their intrinsic motivation for putting in effort and going deeper with their learning.

Make the connection between classroom activities and real-world situations

Maybe one of your students wants to be an engineer when they grow up. If so, they need to have a solid understanding of math concepts. Knowing that what they're studying will help them meet their goals in the future will boost your students' intrinsic motivation.

Get out of the way

Trust your students to find their own way as often as possible. Your work as a teacher is to lay the groundwork and provide a framework for the work to be done. Independent practice is critical to learning, and offering too much help is often more problematic than not giving enough.

MAINTAIN HIGH EXPECTATIONS

There is often a perception that trauma-informed, resilience-focused education means there is no discipline and low expectations. This seems to be the most difficult for educators new to this approach. This could not be farther from the truth. This approach doesn't mean kids do whatever they want, or that there aren't consequences.

Use students as resources – when they fall below expectations, ask them what they need to be supported. When you are using standards, focus on the standard, not the specific task. Differentiate by interest/choice. Some students may work better individually, while others work best in a group.

Language:

- "Of course you will meet the standard, I just need to explain it in a new way."
- "How can you show me you meet the standard?"
- "You aren't there yet..." (growth mindset)
- "Do your best."
- "What can I do to support you?"

IN-SCHOOL SUSPENSION

Many schools, especially those at the elementary and junior high levels, have rooms designated for students who have been sent out of the classroom due to behavioral problems. Often times, these rooms are named in a way that sounds positive and strength-based, but in reality what happens in this space is far from it. Some of these rooms are used in a punitive manner, staffed by individuals that purposely carry an upset, disappointed, or even angry disposition. They often lecture students about their behavior and then dole out negative consequences. Some schools have recognized that this negative tone is not supported by research, so the space becomes a place where students are expected to sit quietly and "cool off" and "think about what they've done". While this is less negative and less punitive, it is far from productive.

Imagine for a moment if we quizzed kindergarten students on their ABCs each morning, and when they were unable to complete them correctly we sent them to a corner to "think about their ABCs and not come back until they can recite them properly". No one would suggest such a silly and counterproductive academic intervention. However, we know that just like reading, writing, and arithmetic, behavior is also learned and needs to be practiced. So why do we send students who show deficits in the area of behavior to a blank room to think about how they need to behave, making the room a miniature version of county jails with miniature versions of county jail inmates? It does not make sense and it is not teaching. If we are going to send students out of the classroom because they are unable to behave in a way that is safe and productive for themselves and other students, the space they are sent to needs to be a safe, supportive learning environment where they learn the behaviors and social and coping skills they need to be successful in class.

WHAT CAN YOU DO?

When we look at children and see behavior as a problem we need to extinguish, we are doing ourselves and especially the child a tragic disservice. It's true the behaviors can be extinguished. We can bribe, threaten, impose, coerce, and break many children to stop doing something or to start doing something. But what have we accomplished?

Notice

Noticing good behavior and providing feedback is essential.

- "Wow, I saw that!"
- "What happened when you _____?"
- "You not only did the problem yourself, but you helped your friend. That's great!"
- "Tell all of us how you did that!"
- "Let's brainstorm as a class – how do you think we should do this...?"
- "Thanks for getting started."
- "Good start, now try to add more details."
- "Can you explain that to me?"
- "You were such a good classmate when you noticed her needing your help."

A Comparison

Punishment and Reward	The Circle of Courage®
Rules	Values
Compliance	Growth
Little educational value	Education potential

If we ascribe to the Circle of Courage® model, we know that the behavior we see is the clue of any one or more unmet needs, and is most likely fueled by pain. So if we extinguish the behavior, have we met the need? Have we soothed the pain? No. The unmet need and the pain still exist. And, as soon as the child is able, they will try to cope again with the pain of the experience of their unmet need. They might choose a more acceptable way to cope, or they may not. In most cases, children escalate to more intense and frequent challenging behaviors. When this happens, the child has not learned ways to get their needs met, and will relapse as soon as bribery, threats, imposition, or coercion is removed. We have found that it works well to assess a child's universal needs according to the Circle of Courage®.

As we reflected early in Step 1, there is no such thing as a bad child. Their behaviors may be bad and challenging, but those behaviors are always a direct response to the pain they are feeling from an unmet need – broken circles. The behaviors are also learned. The environment in which a child develops determines which need is met/unmet, and corresponding copings are learned. Therefore, it is not, "What is wrong with this child?" but rather, "What is wrong with this environment, what has happened, what continues to happen, and what support is needed?"

> When a flower doesn't bloom, you fix the environment in which it grows, not the flower."
>
> – *Alexander Den Heijer*

Universal Needs Assessment Self-Report
Page 1 of 2

The universal needs for all individuals are belonging, mastery, independence, and generosity.

Child's Name_____ Date _____

Directions: In each of the categories check each box that you believe applies to you.

🔺 BELONGING

Family
- ☐ I get along well with my parent/caregiver.
- ☐ My parent/caregiver wants to know where I am.
- ☐ I feel very close to at least one adult.
- ☐ My family often shows that they love me.

School
- ☐ I feel like I belong in school.
- ☐ Individuals feel like they belong at school.
- ☐ Teachers treat me fairly.
- ☐ There is at least one adult in school I trust.

Peers
- ☐ I have a close friend I can trust.
- ☐ My friends accept kids who are different.
- ☐ My parents approve of most of my friends.
- ☐ Most kids I know are kind to others.

☐	Total number checked BELONGING

INDEPENDENCE

Self-Regulation
- ☐ I can keep calm when I get overwhelmed.
- ☐ I control my temper and emotions.
- ☐ I am learning to think before I act.
- ☐ My sense of humor gets me through hard times.

Self-Efficacy
- ☐ I am confident and feel in charge of my life.
- ☐ I can give my opinion even if others disagree.
- ☐ I don't easily get discouraged if things go wrong.
- ☐ If I have a problem or conflict, I usually can solve it.

Self-Discipline
- ☐ I think for myself and am not easily misled by peers.
- ☐ I usually get along well with the person in charge.
- ☐ I can stick to a difficult task.
- ☐ I am developing life goals and planning my future.

☐	Total number checked INDEPENDENCE

Universal Needs Assessment Self-Report
Page 2 of 2

🏹 MASTERY

Strengths

☐ I usually pay attention in school.

☐ I try to learn from my mistakes.

☐ I am curious to learn new things.

☐ People can become smart by studying and practicing new skills like math, reading, and writing.

Supports

☐ My family is very interested in my school success.

☐ My friends encourage me to do my best in school.

☐ My teachers expect me to work hard and succeed.

☐ My school has many opportunities for learning.

Engagement

☐ Most of my school subjects are interesting.

☐ I participate in one or more of the following: sports, music, art, or hobbies.

☐ I like to read, even outside of school.

☐ School teaches me skills that will be useful later in life.

_____

☐ Total number checked MASTERY

❤️ GENEROSITY

Empathy

☐ It bothers me when people are mean to others.

☐ If I do things that hurt others, I feel bad afterwards.

☐ I can usually understand what others are feeling.

☐ I can see another's point of view.

Altruism

☐ I help a lot at home and with my family members.

☐ If my friends are upset, I usually try to help them.

☐ I try to forgive others rather than hold a grudge.

☐ I like to volunteer to help others.

A Caring Community

☐ In my family, we help one another through hard times.

☐ Adults in my school really care about their students.

☐ Individuals try to help others and make all feel welcome.

☐ No one has the right to hurt anyone, and all should help.

_____

☐ Total number checked GENEROSITY

REPETITION

Sometimes we put a plan in place and only try it a few times, or for a short period of time, before we decide, "It doesn't work". What we know about working with traumatized students is that we need to give things time, re-evaluate often, and track progress. Remember, you are providing the student with a new experience to create a new pathway deep in their brain. This takes time. Progress is always more important than perfection. When behavior difficulties are less frequent, less intense, and are shorter in duration, that is progress and we should look at this growth as success. When working in an environment daily, it can be easy to only see what is left to be done. When you see difficult behavior or students hurting, we can become overwhelmed.

Tips
- Notice where student was and where they are now.
- Use data to provide feedback, not as a reward.
- Say things like, "Wow, that is a new thing!"

POSITIVE BEHAVIOR INTERVENTION SUPPORT

Trauma-informed, resilience-focused schools, look at the needs of each child. Therefore, PBIS can be integrated into trauma-informed, resilient schools, but it should be done with a focus on relationships, self-awareness, and regulation rather than on rewards and punishments.

Positive
- Positive reinforcement through encouraging feedback and noticing.
- Connect with students.
- Build relationships – not just rapport.
- Search for and build upon student strengths and interest.
- Assess for each student's universal needs indicating which needs are being met and those which not being met.
- Don't just reward a few. Celebrate the entire class for effort.

Behavior

- Use behavior as your clue.
- Behavior is a response to unmet needs and/or a survival response.
- Be curious about behavior.
- Ask "What might be driving this behavior?"
- Ask "What might the child's private logic be, and how is that impacting the behavior?"

Intervention

- Intervention is not for tracking negative behaviors.
- Use Starr's Behavior Support Plan to support the Circle of Courage® universal needs of belonging, mastery, independence, and generosity.

Support

- Adapt the environment to support the student.
- Provide calming corners.
- Use sensory supports, mentors, reset spaces, restorative practices, brain breaks, and play.

RECOGNIZE CLASSROOM TRIGGERS

These are the most common classroom triggers for students of all ages.

• Conflict

Even when a child is not directly involved, witnessing conflict (physical or verbal) can be a trigger for fight, flight, and freeze responses.

• Being provoked

This will immediately trigger a fight response in most children. Remember that being provoked can come in the form of verbal or non-verbal "attacks".

- **Pressure**

Students perceive pressure in various ways including:

- Being rushed.
- Other students understand class content better than them.
- When called on by the teacher.
- When asked to work in a group.
- Talking in front of the class.
- Deadlines.
- Not understanding verbal directives.
- Frustration.
- Ineffective problem solving.
- Academic errors.
- Peers don't understand student.
- Teacher doesn't understand student.
- Unable to articulate what student wants to say.

SETTING UP STUDENTS FOR SUCCESS

Preventative Interventions:

- Remove student from, or modify the trigger.
- Redirect behavior by providing reasonable choices/options for alternative activities.
- Anticipate problem behavior and intervene before it starts.
- Notice signs of distress.
- Connect with the student.
- Know your students and set them up to succeed, instead of waiting for them to "fail" or become dysregulated.
- Pay attention to the classroom environment and how it might make an impact on students who are vulnerable to triggers (noise, light, smells, crowds, changes in schedule).
- Relaxation techniques.
- Pre-arranged signal between student and teacher.
- Emphasize student choices and responsibilities in clear and simple language.

- Time in (see next section).
- Avoid escalation responses.
- Avoid yelling/raising voice.
- Avoid getting too close.
- Avoid power struggle.
- Avoid discrediting student.

YOUR PHYSIOLOGY IMPACTS THEIR PHYSIOLOGY

- Lower the volume and pitch of your voice.
- Slow down your speech and pause between sentences.
- Slow down your body movements.
- Only after the student is calm, discuss what happened.

A 10th grade girl in my class was physically abused by her dad. How do I balance her need for support with the comfort level of her classmates? She's been sharing a lot of details with other kids in class, and I can see it's making them feel uncomfortable. I want to support her, but I also want to help her understand when it is appropriate to share.

This type of situation can leave teachers feeling torn: you want to help the student who is suffering, but you also want to make sure the other students are comfortable in your classroom. It's best to be direct. You want to protect the girl who was abused, but you also need to protect the other kids. Take her aside discretely and let her know it's appropriate to share with a very close friend who desires to listen, a teacher, or counselor, but it is not appropriate to share with everyone. When other students hear the details, they may perceive it can possibly happen to them, which can cause post-traumatic stress reactions in those students too. It doesn't have to actually happen to them for it to worry them. If other kids are complaining, let them know they can come to you if she shares too much with them. They have a right to not be exposed to the discussion. Even though this may feel like a difficult conversation to have with a student, it will help her—as well as the rest of your class—feel safe and supported.

FLOWCHART STEPS DEFINED

Remember: A trauma-informed and resilience-focused approach to a student who is "off-task" should involve the educator asking themselves these four key questions before approaching the student to help.

1 Am I currently able to regulate my own emotions and behavior?
2. Which one or more of this student's universal needs is lacking right now? (belonging, mastery, independence, generosity)
3. How can I help this student regulate his emotions and/or behavior in this moment?
4. How can I make this a learning opportunity for this student?

CLASSROOM TIER I SUPPORTS

Remember the Tier 1 Circle of Courage® supports . Review those found in Step 1.

In-class Reset: NOT a PUNISHMENT

- A space in the room that may include a rug, pillow, drawing materials, headphones, fidgets, timer, and other calming activities.
- Teach (introduce, model, practice) all students how to use reset spaces in the room before needed.
- Ask student if the reset space would help.
- NEVER SEND a student to the reset space. It is ALWAYS a choice.

RESETTING FOR RESILIENCE FLOWCHART

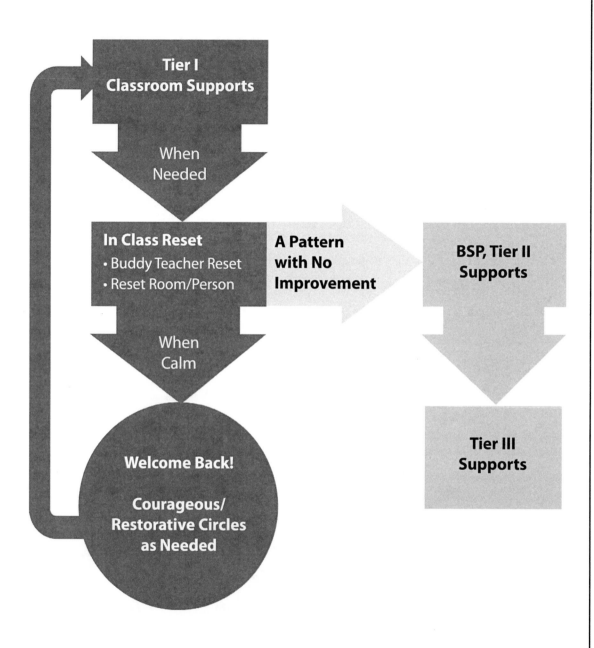

Tier I Classroom Supports

When Needed

In Class Reset
• Buddy Teacher Reset
• Reset Room/Person

A Pattern with No Improvement

When Calm

Welcome Back!

Courageous/ Restorative Circles as Needed

BSP, Tier II Supports

Tier III Supports

Although exclusive practices are not on the chart, there may be some extreme safety-related circumstances that may be used while plans are developed to meet a student's needs and provide safety.

Buddy Teacher/Staff Reset: NOT a PUNISHMENT

- A reset space is a prearranged classroom/place the student can go to reset. It is staffed by a buddy teacher, a SAFE person the student trusts.
- The buddy teacher/staff welcomes the student, and calls the student's teacher to let them know the student arrived.
- The buddy teacher/staff also calls the student's teacher when the student is ready to return to class.

Reset Room/Space: NOT A PUNISHMENT

- It is a predetermined (practice ahead of time) place the student can go to reset.
- It is not a punishment, but a place to regain control.
- When the student is calm, someone is available for them to talk to, if needed.
- It gives a chance to practice some mind/body skills.
- It gives a chance to role play.
- It gives a chance to make a plan to fix any harm done.

WELCOME BACK

Teacher asks themselves the four key questions on page 153 and gets ready to greet the student. Teacher smiles, nods, and is welcoming to the student when they return. The goal is to HELP the student be successful when they return.

The teacher may say...

- "Welcome back."
- "Let me know if you need anything."
- "Trevon, can you help (student who reset) get caught up on what we're doing?"
- "We can talk later (give specific time) if you would like to."
- "I'm sorry...." (if needed.)
- Follow up with buddy teacher or anyone else involved.
- Follow up with student one on one if needed.

Courageous/Restorative Circle

- May involve student and teacher, student and peer, student-teacher-peer/s, entire class, or anyone affected.

- Courageous Proactive Circles should already be implemented and practices on a regular basis.
- Problem/concern is written in agenda or put into "Problem/Concern" box.
- Problem/concern brought up at meeting reminding that we are focusing on HELPING to meet Universal Needs.
- Solutions brainstormed by all concerned parties.
- Solutions chosen by affected parties, and may include a restoration plan if needed.
- Follow up at a later date to see if problem is resolving or needs to be revisited.

RESTORATION PLAN

Individualized plan agreed upon by all parties that may include fixing any harm done. It is imperative that the harmer and those harmed develop and agree on the plan. Teaching students how to solve problems and restore relationships on their own is one of the main goals!

Examples include:

- Replacing/repairing damaged items or giving up free time to work to replace them.
- Spending time with harmed parties to develop a better relationship.
- Apologizing and asking for forgiveness.
- Identifying ways to meet unmet needs (see Universal Needs Assessment).

ALL OF THE PROACTIVE STRATEGIES SHOULD BE IN PLACE WITH 100% FIDELITY! THESE PRACTICES HELP ALL STUDENTS ALL OF THE TIME.

Remember this sobering reality. There are two types of students who enter your school:

1. Those who are loved at home, and really don't need a whole lot from you. Generally speaking, they are going to learn and do well regardless.
2. And then there's those who need you desperately. The ones who struggle a lot. All too often, these are the ones we push away.

In-class Reset is NOT a PUNISHMENT

- A space in the room that may include a rug, pillow, drawing materials, headphones, fidgets, timer, and other calming activities.
- Teach (introduce, model, practice) all students how to use reset spaces in the room before needed.
- Ask student if going to the reset space would help them.
- Never SEND a student to the reset space. It is ALWAYS a choice.

In-class reset spaces can include:

- Pillows and cushions
- Stuffed animals
- Lava lamps
- Ear "mufflers"
- Play-doh or modeling clay
- Sand tray
- Rocking chair
- Art/coloring supplies

- Exercise balls
- Bubble machines
- Bean bags
- Beads and string
- Fish tank
- Mini-trampoline
- Activity sheets

- Weighted blankets
- Sound machines
- Fidget toys
- Headphones with music
- Sunglasses and hats
- Swings
- Word searches

If the in-class reset doesn't work, it means the student needs more time to regulate.

- Remember, a reset space is not a punishment!
- A reset space is a prearranged classroom/place the student can go to reset, staffed by a buddy teacher or a SAFE person the student trusts.
- The buddy teacher/staff welcomes the student, and calls the student's teacher to let them know the student arrived and calls when the student is ready to return to class.

When the in-class or buddy teacher reset works, then the student can resume normal classroom activities. If they still need support, move to Tier II supports....

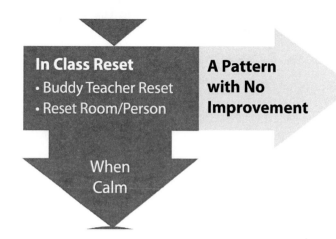

In Class Reset
- Buddy Teacher Reset
- Reset Room/Person

A Pattern with No Improvement

When Calm

**Trauma-Informed, Resilience-Focused
Behavior Support Plan for Children and Adolescents
For Schools and Agencies**

This Behavior Support Plan will help you maintain a strength-based, nonpunitive approach to working with youth in all settings. This Support Plan is trauma-informed and resilience-focused, and will help you observe behavior with curiosity, exploring not only the behavior itself but the underlying causes for it. It does not focus on changing behaviors, but rather on providing what is needed based upon the student's private logic and unmet universal needs. This resource will guide you through the assessment and behavior support plan writing process.

This 19 page PDF download includes our Behavior Support Plan and Universal Needs Assessment forms. You can complete the forms on your computer or print them out. Either way, you can use the forms over and over again with each of your clients.

Ages: elementary through high school.
19 pages
Published by: Starr Commonwealth

TIER II SUPPORTS
COMPLETE A TRAUMA-INFORMED, RESILIENCE-FOCUSED BEHAVIOR SUPPORT PLAN

Notify Parent(s)/Caregiver

When possible, frame accordingly:

- What the underlying private logic or unmet need causing the behavior appears to be
- As a result, what the behavior has been
- What is going to be done to help their child
- Ask for input

Communicating with a student's parent or caregiver is essential. Share examples of the private logic and universal need assessments you have completed for their child. Highlight how private logic and deficits in any one or more of the student's universal needs such as experiencing belonging, mastery, independence, and generosity often leads to problematic and challenging behavior. Explain how you will provide experiences so that the child can begin to have these needs met which will help improve the child's ability to succeed in the school setting. Remind parents and caregivers that their child will need to experience having their universal needs met several times before changes may be noticed. If there is still no improvement after several weeks of providing such supports, move to Tier III interventions.

BSP, Tier II Supports

TIER III SUPPORTS

"Jamar, a kindergarten student, got so angry he hit and punched a peer. His teacher walked him into the hall and he sat on her lap and she rocked him until he calmed down. Then, he returned to class and worked things out with the victim. She practiced having him come to her when he started feeling angry so she could help him regulate by holding him or having him near her. When he was calm, he would often tell her things that were triggering him."

Reset Rooms

- Reset can be done anywhere outside of the classroom.
- Reset rooms may also be referred to as the Wellness Center or Restore Room.
- Reset rooms should be utilized only after in-class resets have been offered.

In-classroom resets include access to tool kits, comfort corners, one-minute interventions, mind/body practices, and walks in the hallway. High quality, self-regulation support strategies in the classroom should reduce the need for out of class resets significantly. Proactive interventions to support the needs of children will also reduce the need for out-of-class resets or further time out of the classroom.

In order for a reset room to be utilized in a trauma-informed way, and truly provide students with tools and skills to cope in the future, it must have the following components:

Sensory-Based

The student must be given the opportunity to be guided through a mind-body practice, a one-minute intervention, or a practice on their own before any conversation is had. The adult will be ready and willing to give the student choice in what they need to practice in order to calm down/deactivate. This is even after the sensory component was offered in the classroom. The adult presence should be focused on re-establishing a sense of safety for the child. Sensory tools and mind-body practices need to be taught in the classroom to ALL students, so when there is an issue, the student already has a reference for practices that support the student in self-awareness and regulation.

Relationship/Restorative Conversation

When (and only when) the student is ready to talk, the restorative conversation can begin.

The adult supporting the student will know the child is ready when they see their breathing slow down, their muscles relax, and their faces soften. The child must also be able to say they are ready to talk. If the child is not ready, they should not be forced. The conversation may need to be offered repeatedly. At no point should the adult lecture or yell at the child.

Ideally, the connection with the student and the adult who is involved in the issue would not be broken at any time in this process. Additionally, this adult would accompany the student through the sensory process, and then be the person participating in the restorative conversation. If this is not possible, the adult that is facilitating the deactivation/sensory process would wait for the student to be ready, and then follow the restorative question script.

Questions to ask...

- What happened, and what were you thinking at the time?
- What have you thought about since?
- Who has been affected by what you have done? In what way?
- What has been hardest for you?
- What do you think you need to do to make things as right as possible?

If the adult who was involved in this process was not able to be a part of the conversation, there will need to be a time set aside for that adult to have a conversation with the child in order to restore that relationship. For example: The classroom teacher was unable to accompany the student to the sensory/reset space outside of the classroom. The student was supported by another adult, and has had a restorative conversation. When the child returns to the classroom, the teacher welcomes them back warmly, trusting that a colleague has supported the student in the process. As soon as possible, the teacher takes time aside with the student, and dialogues with them following the restorative script. At times, if the incident has impacted the whole classroom, there may need to be a restorative circle held for the whole class.

Environment

The reset space should be relaxing, inviting, and have therapeutic attributes. For example, the space can include calm lighting, relaxing music, snacks, water, comfortable seating, or aromatherapy. It should not feel like a punitive space. Activities in the room should be quiet and reflective. There could be a writing space, an art space, sensory tools (squeeze balls, fidgets, breathing balls, textured fabrics, hammocks, yoga mats, core stabilizing balls, etc.)

Staff

Teachers and staff must be trained in trauma-informed and restorative practices. Administration must openly support their staff with all aspects of this process, require that all staff adhere to these practices, and be trained in and model the practices as well.

In-School Suspension

Ideally we would re-name ISS. It could be called Extended Pause Space, or Extended Interval Breathing Space.

If the student is not ready to participate in the restorative conversation and be part of strategizing ways to make it right, it may be that they need to spend extended time in school, but outside of the classroom. While the student is in the room, an adult should be available to continue to offer a restorative conversation anytime the student is ready. To keep this process trauma-informed, it is imperative that the student never feel isolated. There should always be a supportive adult present who is able to look through the curious trauma-informed lens and assess the student's needs by interacting with them to find out what is happening.

Environment

This space should not be punitive. Too often these spaces are made to feel like the school jail. This is not a trauma-informed environment. The ISS space could also be the reset space, if that makes sense for the particular building/staffing needs. The lighting should be calm, calming music could be an option, and seating should be comfortable. All components of the reset space should be available to the child so they have resources to support self-regulation. The layout of the room should allow space for reflection, but not create space that feels isolated. Yoga mats and pillows on the floor, or circular tables, provide the child with a space to reflect without being shut off from the room. This allows the student to connect with the adult in the room to initiate the restorative process when they are ready.

Activities

Reflective spaces would be offered for the student to be guided through social/emotional curriculum that is relevant and developmentally appropriate to the issue that brought us to this point. Writing "I will not....." sentences repeatedly is not a trauma-informed practice and would not be used here. Allowing the student to write or draw to express how they are feeling now is much more supportive to restoring the student's relationship with themselves and their teacher/classroom.

If this cannot be resolved by the end of the school day, a group of people should be scheduled to meet before the start of the following school day in order to establish a support plan and create time for a restorative conversation between the people involved. If a student is needing to spend time out of the classroom frequently, the classroom teacher, principal, and support staff need to meet and design an intervention plan for the student in order to better meet the student's needs. The Circle of Courage® support plan tool would be very useful here.

Role of Reset Room Staff

- Assess student's private logic and identify needs based upon that private logic.
- Assess for broken parts of the student's circle of universal needs.
- Based upon broken circle components, identify interventions to mend those areas.
- Effectively collaborate with students. Provide the opportunity to de-escalate and redirect, followed by practices to re-learn and role play desirable classroom behaviors. Also, help students complete the work they are missing in class through direct instruction.
- Encourage personal reflection and body awareness.
- Identify and practice coping strategies.
- Help student to keep school work organized, assist them in completing it, empower them to take risks but to feel comfortable asking for help when needed.
- Give one assignment at a time rather than a stack of assignments for the day.
- Provide supportive materials.
- Maintain communication among teachers, parents, and administrators.
- Role play and practice pro-social behaviors.
- Develop a plan WITH the student, and any hurt parties, to restore relationships or repair harm. This may include: community/school service hours (peer tutoring, clean up, helping a teacher with copying, sorting papers, etc.).
- Be the student advocate.

How Should the Room Look?

- Size of the room – regular classroom size.
- If it is too large, its implications are that the room will accommodate many students. If the space is too small, however, it could feel jail-like and most likely will not be able to store all of the supplies and materials necessary for students to accomplish their work.

Arrangement

- Desks pushed together or in circles to facilitate connections and discussion.
- Staff in resource room should sit with the students, not in a "power" position.

Colors

- Do not use black, white, beige, or gray paint colors.
- To decrease stress, use warmer reds, peachy orange, warmer yellow, salmon, lavender, and soft blue.

PRIORITY IN THE RESET ROOM: Cool Down

- Assesses body language and intervene accordingly.
- Remain calm and therapeutic in verbal and non-verbal disposition.
- Give time and space as needed.
- Tell student that you are there to help and will do so when they are ready.
- Offer choices (i.e., sensory interventions).
- Refrain from asking too many questions, lecturing, or forcing student to complete forms, homework, etc.

RESOURCES IN THE RESET ROOM

- Tight-fitting vests
- Headphones for music or nature sounds like rain/water
- Headphones to block out sound
- Large-lined paper
- Dimmer lighting
- Weighted objects, vests, stuffed animals, or blankets to set on lap, shoulders, or hands
- Taping a strip of texture (Velcro, bristles from a paint brush, smooth-slick surfaces, mild sand paper, rubber, cloth, etc.) on or underneath desks, on pencils, or other objects.
- Weighted pencil ends or erasers
- Rubber pencil grips
- Fidget toys
- Air seat pads
- Sitting on a yoga ball
- Rocking chair
- Textured paper or raised lines
- Tilted desk top
- Chewing gum
- Mini Spectra light globe
- Mini lava lamp
- Silly putty/Theraputty/Thinking putty
- Moldable erasers
- Floam
- Slime/Flubber
- Play-Doh
- Slinky
- Bubble wrap
- A bin with different various pieces of textured fabric
- Containers of rice, beans, sand, noodles, etc.
- Pillows
- Scented markers and stickers
- Mini trampoline
- Wiggle/balance board
- Heavy lifting class/school jobs and tasks
- Frequent activities/assignments that incorporating feeling and touching things
- Incorporating relevant sounds into assignments, lessons, activities, etc.
- Activities, assignments, and tasks incorporating visual tracking
- Magnifying glasses
- *Mind Body Skills** activity worksheets
- *One Minute Trauma Interventions**
- *More One Minute Trauma Interventions*
- *Healing the Experience of Trauma: A Path to Resilience Program**

*Available for purchase at: store.starr.org.

GOOD RESTORATIVE CIRCLE EXAMPLES

"Chasity, 4th grade, stole from other students. She stole their erasers, pencils, snacks, etc. Her peers were angry, rejecting, and blamed her any time something was missing. She even stole a notepad from the Scholastic Book Fair. We held a class meeting and discussed ways we could HELP Chasity. The students came up with lots of ideas, "She could ask to use it, she could earn some money and buy it, etc." Many students told of stories when THEY had stolen something, and the teacher did, too. Chasity could feel that her peers were really trying to help her. She told the class a story about how she had stolen something from a store, and her parents had locked her in her room for a long time (we reported this and talked to the parents about it). Chasity said she was sorry and returned many of the missing items. She worked off the amount she owed for the notepad by cleaning off the tables in the cafeteria for a week and apologizing to the librarian. She "borrowed" some items without asking for a while, and we addressed it in later meetings, but little by little, she completely stopped stealing."

"Caleb, 4th grade, was scared of Mr. Snyder, the gym teacher. He said he always yelled at him. We invited Mr. Snyder to our class meeting and I told him that some of the students were afraid to go to gym because they thought he was mad at them. He listened and explained his side. He only has 45 minutes to go over all the expectations, etc. and wants them to have time to do the activity, so if they are goofing around he gets frustrated and yells sometimes. After hearing all sides, both Mr. Snyder and the students came up with some solutions that all could agree on."

"Curtis, 5th grade, made some sexual remarks to a few girls in class. During the class meeting, girls gave examples of how it made them feel when boys made inappropriate comments to them and how they didn't like it. Some boys talked about how they'd seen men talk mean to their moms and how they didn't like it. We practiced some other ways that Curtis could get a girl's attention without offending her. Curtis apologized and agreed to try other ways to get a girl's attention."

Debate	VS.	Dialogue
Persuade		Listen to learn
Achieve a specific goal		Understand to be understood
Search for flaws		Explore others thoughts, views, beliefs
Defend		Build relationships
Win an argument		Expand views
Give specific solution		Get meaning behind words
Judgmental		Non-judgmental
Opposing teams		Same team
May not value or respect others		Value and respect all

Benefits

- Give victims a chance to express their feelings directly to offenders, supported by family/friends.
- Let offenders hear directly from the people they have affected.
- Hold offenders accountable.
- Empower offender to take responsibility for their actions.
- Provides an opportunity for healing.
- Works toward reintegrating offenders back into their community (school, classroom, etc.).
- Break cycles of misbehavior and disruption.

Intervene (Reset Room)

- Intervention is ALWAYS individualized to the student (based on assessment).
- Intervention tools (e.g., *One Minute Interventions, MORE One Minute Interventions, Mind Body Skills: Activities for Emotional Regulation, Healing the Experience of Trauma, 10 Steps to Create a Trauma-Informed Resilient School*, etc. available for purchase at: store.starr.org.).
- Life/social skills and/or anger management instruction and practice.
- Strength-based restorative dialogue and reframing.
- Teaching and discussing patterns of behavior.
- Deciding upon and practicing 1-3 strategies at a time.
- Time and assistance for completion of academic work.
- Group/peer mentoring and conflict resolution.

NOTE: If student refuses, they may need more cool down time or sensory intervention

Restore (from Reset Room)

- Once staff member thinks the student might be ready to return to class, they ask the student if they are ready.
- If the student says they are not ready, staff member asks them what they still need in order to be ready to return to class and be successful. Revisit/practice intervention strategies OR work on academics that are being missed, depending on the answer given by the student.
- If it becomes clear that the student is avoiding class, explore with the student what it is exactly they are trying to avoid and help them problem-solve the situation.
- If the student says they are ready to return to class, the administrator who referred them to the reset room is notified. Administrator then checks in with student to make sure they agree that they are ready and that all expectations have been met. If so, administrator checks in with the teacher (without the student present) to make sure the teacher is ready to receive them in a restorative, strength-based manner.
- When the student is brought to the classroom, if needed, the teacher steps into the hallway and a brief restorative discussion is facilitated. If more intervention/time is needed, this conversation can take place during the teacher's next prep period.

Restore (from Office)

- Ask the student if they feel ready to return to class.
- If they are not, revisit/practice intervention strategies OR work on academics being missed and give more time.
- If it becomes clear that the student is avoiding class, explore with student what it is exactly they are trying to avoid and help them problem-solve the situation.
- If the student says they are ready to return to class, check in with receiving teacher (without student present) to ensure the teacher is ready as well.
- When the student returns to the classroom, if needed, a brief restorative discussion is facilitated away from other students. If more intervention/time is needed, this conversation can take place during the teacher's next prep period.

Suspension (Last Resort)

Only occurs in situations where physical structure and safety needs to be established.

- Bringing weapons
- Creating extreme danger at school

Suspension should be used only as a last resort, as it should be avoided with focus on staff/student relationships and restorative processes used with fidelity. We believe suspension should only occur in situations where physical safety and structure needs to be established. Examples of these situations are bringing weapons or creating extreme danger at school. The student should have high quality interventions in place that are implemented consistently, and have been through the process of in-class and out-of-class reset/restorative processes before suspension should even be considered. If a student must be suspended due to severe safety issues, a support team for that student must meet to create a support intervention plan for the child when they return to school. The child and parents must be included in this plan and be asked for input to accurately inform the team of the needs of the child. A restorative circle must be held prior to the child returning to school in order to reintegrate the student into the school community. A classroom circle may need to be held as well. While the student is out of school, the teacher should call the student every day to check on the child and reassure the child they are still part of the classroom community. A home visit would be optimal.

Restore (from Home)

- Administrator AND teacher check in with student and parent(s)/caregiver DAILY while out-of-school.
- Genuinely convey to student and parent(s)/caregiver that student is WANTED back in school.
- When student returns, administrator AND teacher meet with student and parent(s)/caregiver to genuinely welcome student back to school and discuss a plan.
- Tell student you want to help them be successful and never have to be out-of-school again.
- Ask student how you and others can help.
- Develop Behavior Support Plan with student.

Welcome Back

Teacher smiles, nods, and is welcoming to the student when they return…

The goal is to HELP the student be successful when they return.

Teacher May Say…

- "Welcome back."
- "Let me know if you need anything."
- Trevon, can you help (student who reset) get caught up on what we're doing?"
- "We can talk later (give specific time) if you would like to."
- "I'm sorry…." (if needed)
- Follow up with buddy teacher or anyone else involved.
- Follow up with student one-on-one if needed.

ACTIVITY:
Reframing Behaviors

How can you reframe the following common statements we hear school professionals make about students so that they are more trauma-informed?

- He loves to push my buttons

_____

_____

- She always has to get her way

_____

_____

- He's better than this

_____

_____

- She isn't even trying

_____

_____

- He ruined it for the rest of the class

_____

_____

- She can't be trusted

_____

_____

- He is just mean

_____

_____

- She is always complaining

_____

_____

- It is like there is nobody home in there

_____

_____

- She can't sit still for 5 minutes

_____

_____

- He can't keep his mouth shut

_____

_____

Remember this...

STEP 7 HIGHLIGHTS

- Set students up for success. Behavior is always a clue to what the child is experiencing at that moment in time. A traumatized child will not use language, logic, or reason. They will react based upon their needs at that time.
- How might a child act when they are feeling:
  - Unsafe
  - Worried
  - Angry
  - Abandoned
  - Bullied
  - Powerless
  - Guilty
  - Not worthy

STEP 8

Partner with Families and Communities

Education is increasingly viewed as a shared responsibility of educators, families, and communities. Schools, parents, and the community should work together to promote the health, well-being, and learning of all students. When schools involve parents and engage community resources, they are able to respond more effectively to the needs of students. Family and community involvements foster partnerships among schools, family, and community groups and individuals. These partnerships result in sharing and maximizing of resources, as well as a strong belief that all families, regardless of level of education, socio-economic status, and race or ethnicity can contribute to all student learning and development. When schools communicate well and often, parents and communities are not only informed but feel like they have an active voices in their school community. Additionally, they build a culture of inclusivity and eliminate feelings of distrust, uncertainty, and hostility. When school leaders communicate effectively, students learn, parents and community members understand and support what the school is doing, and the process of teaching and learning moves forward. But when educators fail to communicate fully, misinformation, misinterpretations, misunderstanding, and mixed messages can cause a system breakdown

The highest performing schools serving at-risk children distinguish themselves by finding innovative ways to connect with parents and community partners (National Association of State Coordination of Comprehensive Education, 2006). Changes in family demographics, demands of professional workplaces, and growing diversity are just a few of the reasons why schools need strong community and family partnerships. Reaching beyond school walls to provide all the support students need is essential. In some schools, this can be the most challenging step to creating a trauma-informed, resilient school. Depending upon your school climate and surrounding community resources, the level of collaboration will vary. If you have difficulties with parent and family collaborations, you are not alone. But don't be discouraged! Many professionals find that they haven't taken the time to think through their current family and community partnership strengths and opportunities. Walking through the activities in this step helps educators become more aware of ways they can engage school families and their community partners.

PARENTS/FAMILIES

The terms "parent" and "family" are used interchangeably and refer to any adult caregiver or group of caregivers who play a role in a child's cognitive, social, and emotional development including grandparents, foster parents, extended family members, or close friends. Parent engagement in child learning improves academic outcomes and benefits social and emotional development. Positive learning outcomes have been found when parents engage with their child's learning at home by reading and playing mathematics games together, communicating high educational expectations, and talking to their children about school activities and interests (Castro et al, 2015; Fox & Olsen, 2014). Another aspect of parents' engagement with their children's learning is involvement and collaboration with their child's school. Optimal learning outcomes occur when key educators and parents form respectful and collaborative partnerships (Fox & Olson, 2014). Parents are more engaged in their child's learning when schools have high expectations for them to be involved.

While levels of parent involvement in schools decrease as children enter their teen years, parent involvement such as volunteering and attending school events continues to have a positive association with adolescent learning outcomes, as well as mental health outcomes. Parent school partnerships are facilitated by positive school climates. Certain aspects of school climate are particularly important for building partnerships, such as parent-teacher relationships.

Parent engagement is highest when teachers have a positive relationship with the child, care about a child's academic development, and are perceived by the parent as approachable and communicating frequently. High levels of parent involvement are also associated with an overall school climate perceived by parents as safe, trustworthy, respectful, friendly, inclusive, and collaborative (Day, 2013; Goldkind & Farmer, 2013).

Students whose parents are involved in their education are more likely to:

- Adapt well to school.
- Attend school more regularly.
- Complete homework more consistently.
- Earn higher grades and test scores.
- Graduate and go on to college.
- Have better social skills.
- Show improved behavior.
- Have better relationships with their parents.
- Have higher self-esteem.
- Have positive attitudes toward school.

WHAT CAN YOU DO?

At the Beginning of the School Year

- Schedule a school tour and an open house for students and families.
- Create a family room, lending library, or resource center for parents to show them they are welcome in the school.

Connect with Parents and Families

- Distribute surveys, conduct interviews, or home visits to learn more about students, their families, and their cultures.
- Host parent support groups to discuss parenting approaches and school issues.
- Create a suggestion box, notepad, or specific email where parents can share their thoughts with the school.
- Make phone calls or send notes home about great things. Make contact when things are going well, not just when something is "wrong". Share good news often.
- Acknowledge how hard parents and families work, and point out all the great things they are doing for their child.

Stay Connected

- Send home monthly interactive homework assignments and ask students to talk with their parents or other family members about what they are studying in class.

- Send home a weekly or monthly newsletter to share information about ongoing lessons, particular skills that are being targeted, upcoming events, and practical tips on how to promote learning at home.

- Send home materials needed to complete assignments in baggies (like glue, scissors, paper, and markers.)

- Send "thank you" cards home (which students can help create) to engage families and express respect and appreciation.

Invite Family Members

- To visit the classroom to share their skills, talents, and expertise with the class.

- To just visit the classroom. Teachers are influential in creating a classroom climate that supports family involvement. Parents who are invited and feel welcomed are more likely to be actively involved in their children's education both at home and at school.

- To attend student presentations that showcase their artwork, research projects, or classroom projects.

- To chaperone field trips.

Special School Events

- Hold a student of the month assembly, create a bulletin board, or schedule a lunch with families.

- Provide workshops for parents and students on course credits and requirements for high school graduation, college financial aid, college entry tests, and career planning.

- Plan a dinner at the school (food trucks or cafeteria style) coupled with a game night.

- Provide exercise or outdoor activities (yoga or Zumba night, obstacle course activity, dance-a-thon, walk-a-thon or a fun run.)

- Schedule an open house to showcase student learning and progress.

- Thank volunteers by hosting an appreciation breakfast or lunch at the end of the school year.

> The family is the expert on the child. The teacher is the expert on the curriculum.

CASE EXAMPLE: MR. CUNNINGHAM

Jimmy was in 8th grade when his mother, after using heroin for several years, had recently and unexpectedly left Jimmy and his father and moved 200 miles away. Despite her addiction, she had been the primary school contact and was inconsistently present at Jimmy's school events. The school social worker attempted to reach out to Jimmy's father, Mr. Cunningham, on a few occasions following the mother leaving. After a few months, Mr. Cunningham finally called back. He agreed to come in to talk to the counselor, but always canceled or just didn't show up. Knowing the importance of parent involvement, the social worker didn't give up. He called Mr. Cunningham and was never upset with him for missing the appointments. Instead he communicated with Mr. Cunningham in a way that showed understanding and compassion. He also talked with him about Jimmy, but didn't press an in-person meeting. He made sure to let him know in what ways Jimmy was doing well, and in ways he could use support from him. He indirectly educated Mr. Cunningham about the importance of his expectations for his son and how his involvement would benefit him. After communicating this way for several months, during one of their calls Mr. Cunningham asked if he could come up to the school sometime to finally meet in-person. The social worker told him he would love that and to stop by anytime. Later that week, Mr. Cunningham came in when he dropped off Jimmy and brought the social worker

> a cup of coffee. All he said was, "thanks - you didn't push me. I just needed some time."

A school climate is created partly through relationships and interactions among all members of a school community (The National School Climate Council, 2016), including students, teachers, parents, and other school professionals. However, those in leadership positions within the school like the principal and president of the Parent Teacher Association (PTA) may be particularly influential in shaping the school's climate when it comes to parent engagement. School principals can play a central role in shaping school climate and facilitating parent engagement in child learning through their leadership style, communication, attitudes, and expectations. Principals who distribute school leadership among parents and teachers are most successful in embedding a whole school vision that values the role of parents (Barr & Saltmarsh, 2014). Parent organizations such as PTAs create channels for principals and teachers to consult with parents and community about their school. Most research looking at parent attitudes towards parent organizations is positive (Pakseresht & Ahari, 2014).

Q I'm having trouble connecting with one of my 3rd grade students, whose family is homeless and lacks support at home. What can I do? Her mother is so overwhelmed that she basically told me she didn't have any energy to help her daughter or care about how she is doing in school. I want to engage and motivate my student, but the mom's attitude is rubbing off on my student.

Try to shift your lens away from what you think is wrong with your student's mom and look at what is currently happening in her world. The mom is in crisis and survival mode. Likely, she does care about her daughter, but her priority is finding them a place to live. Find a time to connect with mom — either by phone or in person. Informally and briefly reframe the daughter's experience for her. Say to her, "I know you care. You have so much going on now, but your daughter needs you to tell her you care about her and that school is important so that she will stay motivated." Then ask her how you can help. Separately, tell the student that you understand her mom is working hard, and it might not seem like she cares, but she really does – and that you do too. Ask her how you can help. You may need to modify homework expectations for a while or set up a peer support person to help her with her assignments. The support and understanding you give to the parent and the student will go a long way. Flexibility here is important.

WHAT PARENTS NEED TO KNOW ABOUT TRAUMA

Parenting kids who are hurting isn't easy. It is even harder when the parents themselves are struggling too. By normalizing their feelings, you can engage parents in ways that allow them to help their children, while also helping themselves.

Normalize Their Feelings

Every parent needs to hear that their job is hard, and that it is normal to get frustrated, angry, tired, and confused. The more you normalize a parent's experience, the less worried and incompetent they will feel. When you tell a parent, "Yes, I get it. I know it is tough," you communicate that you are there to help, not to gang up on them. This message also lets them know that they are not inadequate; they are doing a challenging job that comes without breaks or vacation time.

Say Things Like:

- "It is normal to get frustrated when everything you do for your child seems to be the wrong thing."
- "A parent isn't being truthful if they tell you that everything is perfect and their kids never act out."
- "This is the hardest job in the world, but nobody can do it better than you."

Empower Them

When you work with parents, come from a place of believing that they know their child better than anyone else. Even if their parenting style differs from yours, let them teach you how it works or makes sense for them. This can be empowering for them, and it communicates that, while you may be a child caring professional, they are the expert when it comes to their child. When a parent who feels powerless is given an opportunity to show what they know about their child, they regain confidence in themselves and in their parenting. When the parent is relaxed and feels heard, they will be better able to attune to their child, which improves their ability to respond appropriately.

Say Things Like:

- "Show me what you find works best when Julia is upset or acts out."
- "What do you think Charlie is trying to tell me when he throws his paper down on the ground?"
- "Is there a certain time of day when John is more tired than other times?"

Trauma is an overwhelming experience for children and parents. Parents want to help their traumatized children, but don't always know what they can do. Providing parents with five ways to help their traumatized children will offer them reassurance for what they are already doing and ideas for how they might be able to do more.

FIVE THINGS PARENTS NEED TO KNOW

1. Understand

Remind parents that trauma is like no other experience. Traumatized children may not have control over their emotions and behavior because the terror they experienced has left them feeling out of control.

2. Be Patient

Trauma destroys a child's sense of safety and security. Children will need time to feel safe again. Be patient with regression.

3. Be Nurturing

This is an "all the cookies and milk you can eat" time. Encourage parents to spend more time with their child interacting in meaningful ways. Play games, read books, or go for a walk together.

4. Keep It Simple

A traumatized child will find it difficult to concentrate and remember even the simplest of

Ideas to collaborate with community partners:

- Student-centered activities
- Scholarships
- Mentoring
- Family counseling
- Beautification projects
- Math, science, art exhibits
- Donation of school materials, equipment, or activities for students and staff
- Provide goods to students
- Tutoring
- Job shadowing
- Family fun nights
- Charitable activities
- Parent workshops and learning opportunities

things. Remind parents to keep things simple by saying only one or two things at a time. Visual charts of the daily schedule or tasks to be completed are helpful.

5. Normalize

Parents need to hear that the reactions their child is experiencing are normal following this experience.

SPOTLIGHT: PARENT ACADEMIES

One trauma-informed school in Detroit, Michigan collaborated with their students' parents by holding Parent Academies several times throughout the school year. The purpose was to provide easy access to education and support for parents.

Topics included: What parents need to know about trauma, How trauma looks like other disorders, Creating the experience of safety with your child, and Fostering connection with your child. The sessions were 90 minutes in length and provided free babysitting so that parents could bring students and siblings if needed. Popcorn, cookies, water, and coffee was provided through a generous sponsorship from the local hospital. The attendance at these sessions was incredible.

ACTIVITY:
What Can Parents Do?

- **What do you think parents can do specifically to build strong bonds with their kids?**

_____

_____

_____

_____

_____

_____

_____

COMMUNITIES

Coordinating resources and services for families, students, and the school with community groups benefits everyone.

Examples of community partners:

- Businesses and corporations
- Universities and educational institutions
- Faith organizations
- National service and volunteer organizations
- Senior citizen organizations
- Cultural and recreational institutions
- Community based organizations
- Individuals

Factors that lead to successful school-community collaboration:

1. School's visible commitment to learning
2. Principal's view of community collaborations
3. Welcoming school climate

Since schools are often regarded as an ideal point of entry to mental health services for children, it is essential for schools to create links to mental health consultation and services for staff, students, and families (Cole et al, 2005). Street outreach programs are also great ways to partner with the community, as they can significantly reduce youth violence. These programs connect trained staff with at-risk youth to conduct conflict mediation, make service referrals, and change beliefs about the acceptability of violence (Davide-Ferdon & Simon, 2014).

INTEGRATION OF BEHAVIORAL HEALTH
INCLUDING TRAUMA ASSESSMENT AND INTERVENTION IN SCHOOLS

Through new strategic partnerships, Starr Commonwealth offers trauma assessment and intervention services to the children who need us most, where access is easiest for them through a school-based mental and developmental health service. Services to children and families include: academic support, family therapy, group therapy, individual and group counseling. All services are rooted in Starr Commonwealth's strength-based, trauma-informed, and resilience-focused philosophy that sees greatness in all children and families. Though grounded in one philosophy, evidence-based interventions employed are individualized to the client-based on needs assessed at intake and throughout treatment as well with cultural and linguistic considerations in mind.

ACTIVITY:
Create an Action Team for Partnerships

Create a resource map to help you pinpoint the opportunities for team partnerships. Here are some ideas on what to include:

- Who are potential community partners, and how can they help support students in your school?

_____

_____

_____

_____

_____

- Ask teachers and students what kinds of community supports they are currently using, as well as resources and collaborations that are needed/wanted.

Consider providing community and school joint professional development opportunities.

The family is the expert on the child. The teacher is the expert on the curriculum.

ACTIVITY:
Your Communities Strengths & Opportunities

List your community strengths and community opportunities:

COMMUNITY STRENGTHS

1. _____

2. _____

3. _____

4. _____

5. _____

6. _____

7. _____

8. _____

9. _____

10. _____

COMMUNITY OPPORTUNITIES

1. _____

2. _____

3. _____

4. _____

5. _____

6. _____

7. _____

8. _____

9. _____

10. _____

**Our community just experienced a tornado. How can I help my students get through this rough time and feel secure again? Many of my students are struggling to find temporary housing. Others are scared whenever the sky looks threatening.**

When an event such as a natural disaster occurs, and is so widespread that it affects the entire community, sometimes there can be a long period of transition where people are out of sorts. Acknowledge to your class that things are not like they were, and as people rebuild or another storm comes, memories can resurface along with feelings of stress. Natural disasters are difficult because they affect a large number of people and the rebuilding process can last a long time. This can lead to chronic stress.

SPOTLIGHT: MARSHALL-ALBION YOUTH SYMPOSIUM

Over 100 middle school students from Albion and Marshall, Michigan participated in a symposium hosted by Albion College and led by Starr Commonwealth. The youth symposium was held after the City of Albion schools were annexed into the Marshall School District to help students from the middle schools of both communities build new and stronger relationships in support of their ongoing education in Marshall.

School & Community Collaboration with a Youth Symposium

Joni Parks, Assistant Superintendent at Albion Community Schools, said: "This was an amazing day for all students and staff involved. The team building activities really changed the awkward climate that we noticed when all the students first arrived today. The Starr staff has done a great job facilitating interactions that not only break the ice, but set the stage for smooth transitions for all students. The panel discussions led by student leaders in Marshall High School were a great outlet for students to express their own fears and reservations about the changes presenting themselves next week at the change of the semester. My students are having a wonderful time, and at supper it was evident that some of those walls are being torn down. Kids from both schools are sitting together and interacting confidently. I am sure all of this will help make that first week of school at Marshall Middle School much easier for the students and staff."

Dr. Randy Davis, Superintendent of Marshall Public Schools, said: "This recent youth symposium on student leadership could not have happened without the ongoing partnership the Marshall Public Schools and Albion Community Schools have had with Starr and Albion College. With less than two weeks to plan, we were able to host over 100 students in grades 6-8 at Albion College for a successful day of coordinated team building experiences and dialogues by Starr. In fact, 20 student leaders at Marshall High School from past youth symposiums volunteered to help make this event a great success. And at the end of the day, the young people participating shared common experiences and found common ground as they prepare to transition into a new middle school learning environment mid-year in Marshall."

Successful school, family, and community partnerships are flexible and diverse, reflecting and incorporating the needs and characteristics of the particular school and community in which they are based. When families, communities, and educators collaborate, they optimize conditions for learning and create opportunities to model and apply communication, behavior, and relationship skills they aim to teach children.

Remember This...

STEP 8 HIGHLIGHTS

- Sometimes engaging parents and the community is the hardest step. Start small and work patiently.
- Students whose parents are involved in their education have higher self-esteem.
- Linking community activities to the classroom improves learning and behavior.

STEP 9

Support and Invest in School Staff

The National School Climate Center notes that "empirical research has shown that when school members feel safe, valued, cared for, engaged, and respected, learning increases and staff satisfaction and retention are enhanced." (2017)

School staff members work hard to ensure the best possible outcomes and experiences for their students. A school leader who routinely recognizes staff members' successes will make all staff feel good and promotes interconnectedness of their work. Celebrating contributions, efforts, and victories make staff feel appreciated and seen. All staff must be recognized. The whole village concept for improving school climate stresses the importance of school employees working together to help students succeed — everyone from administration to support staff. The objective is to create a school culture that thrives.

The rates of teachers leaving the teaching profession are growing. The first five years of a teacher's career may be a time of particular vulnerability, with estimates of 40-50% of early career teachers in many countries leaving the profession during that time. Studies exploring why teachers leave have pointed to teacher stress, burnout (Kyriacou, 2011), and the reality of teacher's work. This step will discuss how supporting staff and trauma-informed schools go hand-in-hand.

All empathetic professionals who are exposed to traumatic situations, either by witnessing them or learning about them from clients, are vulnerable to compassion fatigue. Compassion fatigue is defined many ways. Essentially, it is extreme physical and emotional exhaustion, specific to trauma and loss, that comes on suddenly and results in a lack of ability to feel and show compassion to and for populations being served. While becoming aware of these feelings is the first step in healing, professionals often have difficulty admitting that they have compassion fatigue-related symptoms and reactions. This is largely due to the guilt they feel about their fatigue.

- Helping professionals who experience compassion fatigue often say, "Who am I to complain?"
- Educators whose students are experiencing tremendous grief, trauma, or devastation might feel guilty about their own symptomology and say, "I should rise above this."
- Professionals sometimes feel that as helpers they should be able to "get over" their exhaustion and help those who need it "more" than they do, often thinking, "My feelings of distress are a sign of weakness."
- Adults who experience tragedy all of the time can feel like they should be strong enough to handle it, especially when those affected "have it much worse." They might think, "If I admit to having a hard time, I will open a door that I don't know how to shut."
- Professionals can be afraid to let their guards down for fear that once they let others see them as vulnerable, they will never be able to manage their overwhelming feelings.

Recognition of symptoms and reactions, such as exhaustion, substance use, fear, and isolation related to compassion fatigue, is the first step professionals need to take as they strive to find the sustainable self-care necessary in order to continue working as helpers.

 **What should I do to work through my 4th graders grief over a student in our school who was killed in a recent car accident? Many students have never known anyone who died – especially someone their own age – but I have to say, neither have I!**

When a tragedy like this happens, teachers are often trying to console their students and forget to take care of themselves. Events like this make everyone feel helpless. While educators try to support students, it is imperative for them to receive support too.

ACTIVITY:
DISTRESS INDICATORS

Distress Indicators	Steps to Alleviate Your Distress

What are your emotional distress indicators?

How can you alleviate your emotional distress?

What are your personal distress indicators?

How can you alleviate your personal distress?

What are your physical distress indicators?

How can you alleviate your physical distress?

What are your work distress indicators?

How can you alleviate your work distress?

SELF-AWARENESS AND SELF-REGULATION

When a person is in a state of stress for an exaggerated and prolonged period of time, their bodies are impacted and so is their ability to think clearly and regulate themselves. Indicators of distress are unique to each individual. If you notice any of the following distress indicators in yourself or the professionals at your school, they may be experiencing more demands than resources. These distress indicators are signs of impending burnout.

SOME DISTRESS INDICATORS

Emotional Distress Indicators

- Anger
- Sadness
- Depression
- Anxiety
- Prolonged grief

Physical Distress Indicators

- Headaches
- Stomachaches
- Fatigue
- Sleep problems
- Over/under eating

Personal Distress Indicators

- Isolation
- Cynicism
- Perfectionism
- Mood swings
- Irritability

Work Distress Indicators

- Avoidance (of tasks, peers, students)
- Missed appointments
- Not returning phone calls, emails
- Tardiness, absenteeism
- Lack of motivation

Distress reactions are normal. They are common for many helping professionals, including educators. Vulnerability to distress indicators increases when professionals work with children, and when they have their own trauma histories. Distress is a natural consequence of caring for, listening to, and helping those who are traumatized, so if school professionals are committed to their work with children, they must be educated about distress indicators, and if they are experiencing them, support must be provided. Exposure to others' trauma can lead to vicarious trauma and compassion fatigue. Identify self-care activities that help you relieve stress (e.g., physical exercise, art, music). Then, practice these activities often.

Resilient teachers have been described as those who have the capacity to thrive in difficult circumstances, are able to empathize with students, restrain negative emotions and focus on the positives, experience a sense of pride and fulfillment, and having an increased commitment to their school and profession (Mansfield et al, 2016). Without an understanding of trauma, its impact on students, and support from their school, educators have a difficult time thriving. Supporting staff can be accomplished in many ways. Encourage awareness of distress indicators. Once there is an awareness, educators can take the steps they need to tend to their symptoms, opening up more opportunities to continue a productive career as a helper.

> "Everyone has a responsibility to help and no one has the right to hurt."

> "Teacher morale, in my experience, is not a function of practices designed to maintain or create it. It's a byproduct of being treated as leaders and being treated with respect. Teacher morale is the end product of empowering teachers to make decisions that affect their lives." (New York school superintendent)

SUPPORT FOR EDUCATORS

Educators are vulnerable to burnout, teacher fatigue, and vicarious trauma. All are normal and natural byproducts of caring for, listening to, and teaching students who experience toxic stress and trauma. The cost of caring comes at a high price if there is not support and self-care in place for educators. Supporting staff is an essential step to creating a trauma-informed school and district.

Teachers and staff should have access to training, resources, and time to maintain self-awareness and regulation. It's important to understand that a student's attitudes and behaviors affect teacher and staff attitudes and behaviors and vice versa. When teachers have positive attitudes and behaviors, it will most likely yield positive results – but this shouldn't be an expectation without support. There should be systems in place that allow teachers to proactively take care of themselves, feel supported by peers and administration, recognize distress indicators, detach after a stressful situation, re-establish the relationship with students when necessary, and to have fun at work.

Administration can also begin to look at other ways to support educators.

- Teacher recognition at the district and building administrator level. It could be based on Starr recommendation, ILT observations, hallway behaviors, or it could be student or peer led. There could be an MVP board where teacher pics are placed.
- Create some district events that celebrate teachers and other district staff for the work they do.
- Allow teachers to have a small refrigerator or coffee pot in their classrooms.
- Trust teachers and help support their needs (emotional and resources).
- The district superintendent should focus on visiting every district school and talk to staff, allow the teachers to ask questions, and provide honest communication.
- Empower teachers to use creativity to reach students and foster connections with them.
- Support teachers in the classroom and give them the training and resources they need to manage classroom climate.
- Provide curriculum time for teachers to focus solely on building relationships.
- Create an evaluation tool for teachers that isn't focused on MAP scores and district assessments. (i.e., A teacher can be highly effective in helping students achieve personal

growth even though that student might not be meeting district growth standards.)

Supporting Staff

• Develop their skills

Everybody who has a job can find ways to perform their tasks better. Work with your fellow administrators to create structures that enable everyone to grow in their ability to meet their responsibilities. This might include bringing in some outside training on the school's main office computer systems, or purchasing equipment that may make it easier to clean a part of the building more efficiently. Regardless of what you do, giving that attention goes a long way in reinforcing to people that they matter to the school.

• Solicit their input

Make it a point to gather input from all school staff on a regular basis.

• Hold recognition events

Finally, make it a point to use formal events to recognize them for their hard work. This could be at a school event or perhaps in a small get-together to public and verbally express your appreciation for all that they do.

Remember, you are not here to rescue or save students. You are here to guide them, to provide as many supports as you can, and to see their greatness.

When teachers stop trusting their abilities, they too are working from a stressed brain and their universal need of mastery is not met. Empower adults to trust themselves. Engage in centering practices/self-care.

HELPING EDUCATORS MANAGE THE WEIGHT OF TRAUMA

Teachers, counselor, and administrators may recognize the cumulative stressors that they face, but they don't always realize that their symptoms are a common reaction to working with traumatized children.

BUILDING A CULTURE OF AWARENESS

School leadership should consider ways to appreciate staff, both publicly and privately. This should not simply be recognizing great work, but also acknowledging that the work is difficult. Schools should connect staff who might be experiencing a high stress load with distress indicators with resources. Make it clear that symptoms are not a sign of weakness, but an indicator that they might need support because they work in a challenging profession.

Peer groups are helpful when trying to address the mental health of educators. Trauma-informed resilient schools will create a regular space every week or month where staff can come together to check in with each other about how they are doing emotionally. The meetings can be supported by a mental health professional, and staff are able to share their experiences, learn strategies for understanding their distress indicators, and gain skills to cope with their stress.

ACTIVITY:
Staff Support

How does your school currently support staff?

_____

_____

_____

_____

Like the importance of social emotional skills in children, teachers with self-awareness and self-management are widely acknowledged in teacher resilience literature (Beltman et al, 2011). In fact, leading scientists in the field of social and emotional learning indicate teachers who have strong social and emotional competencies are less likely to experience burnout because they're able to work more effectively with challenging students – one of the main causes of burnout. Educators with social emotional competencies also create classroom climates that students experience as safe because the environments are rich with communication, problem-solving, and lessons that are designed to engage students. Educators with great social-emotional skills are high in both self and social awareness. They recognize and are in control of their own emotions. They understand how what they say or do impacts others, allowing them to create strong relationships with students, colleagues, and parents. They are consistently kind and generous to others (Masfield et al, 2016).

RISK & PROTECTIVE FACTORS FOR TEACHER STRESS

(Prilleltensky, Neff & Bessell, 2016)

Level: Personal

Risk Factors	Protective Factors
• Isolation	• Support network
• Inadequacy	• Mentor match in same teaching area outside of school
• Anxiety	• Participation in indication programs
• Students	• Professional development
	• Safe friend or mentor
	• Self-efficacy
	• Proper nutrition, sleep, exercise
	• Organizational skills
	• Engagement in well-being activities
	• Acceptance, mindful meditation, growth mindset
	• Classroom management
	• Student voice

Level: Interpersonal

Risk Factors	Protective Factors
• Parents • Colleagues	• Regular communication • Parents as partners • Minimize competition • Sharing • Caring and compassion

Level: Organizational

Risk Factors	Protective Factors
• Role Clarification • Disempowering policies and practices	• Definition of principal's expectations • Workload clarification • Create participatory structures • Enhance teacher control of policies • Increase teacher voice and choice

The definition of stress is a condition of the feeling experienced when a person perceives demands to exceed resources.

ACTIVITY:
Your Internal and External Resources

Identify some of your internal and external resources. Some are listed for you. Reflect for a minute about how you use these resources as protective factors. Are there other ways you could draw upon your internal or external resources to help you?

Internal Resources

- Strength
- Humor
- Memories
- Intelligence

- Agility
- Spiritual practice
- Instinct
- Inherent talents

- _____
- _____
- _____
- _____

_____

_____

_____

External Resources

- Nature
- Community
- Hobbies/activities
- Sports/exercise

- Friends
- Animals/pets
- Work
- Family

- _____
- _____
- _____
- _____

_____

_____

_____

CASE EXAMPLE: KENDRA

Kendra is a 3rd year 5th grade school teacher. When she began teaching, she was energetic and full of new ideas. She would often spend her weekends putting together lesson plans and preparing for activities. Since then, she had a baby who is now 18 months old, her husband started a new job requiring a lot of travel, and her class size has grown by 8 students to a total of 26. She feels overwhelmed and exhausted. She wants to love her job again and have energy to spend quality time with her daughter.

Kendra completed an assessment of her internal and external resources and two resources stood out: inherent talents, and her dad, who had always been a great support to her.

It occurred to her that she loved being creative, and that preparing for classroom activities was actually fun for her — not a chore. This simple reframe of a task from "I have to do this" to "I want to and enjoy doing this" helped her see it from a new perspective.

She also realized how much fun her dad had with her daughter, and asked him if he would pick her daughter up from daycare once in a while or watch her on the weekend so that she could spend time catching up on grading or for her own self-care. He responded, "I can't think of anything better I'd like to do."

While her class size didn't change, her attitude towards work did. And she also felt a little bit less overwhelmed with the extra support her dad provided with childcare.

TEACHER BUDDIES

In one school, each teacher paired up with another educator for those moments they needed a break. In this case, they created a protocol to use when a specific student was starting to frustrate them or causing them to feel agitated. They would simply text the student's first name to their designated partner. Then, that other staff would come to their classroom and ask to take the identified student to their classroom for a few minutes "to help with a job" or "give them advice on a certain lesson they were working on".

ACTIVITY:
Reflection Questions

1. Why did you make the decision to do this work? Is that reason the same today, or has it changed over time? Explain.

_____

_____

2. What are your professional strengths?

_____

_____

3. What is your philosophy of what it means to teach students?

_____

_____

_____

4. What aspect of your job is most challenging?

_____

_____

_____

5. Do you need more support to be your best self professionally? If so, what do you need? Who can help?

---

6. If you could choose one or two words about how it makes you feel to do the work you do, what one or two words would you select?

Remember this...

STEP 9 HIGHLIGHTS

- Trauma-informed resilient schools allow for several opportunities for peer collaboration
- Staff need their emotional tanks filled, and filled often!

STEP 10

Collect and Utilize Outcome Data

Creating trauma-informed resilient schools is a process, and outcome data helps show changes in that process. For example, if you don't have baseline data, you won't be able to see how things are changing over time as you implement new trauma-informed practices. This is why we created Starr's *Trauma-Informed School Questionnaire* (TISQ). Starr's TISQ can be given to school staff, families, and students. The questions within each domain of the questionnaire will help you determine which specific area(s) of creating trauma-informed schools are well developed or present an opportunity for enhancement within your school. The TISQ provides a score within each domain/subscale and an overall score along with explanations of how to interpret the scores. The goal is to see improvement. We recommend providing this evaluation tool to staff, families, and students regardless of where you are in the process. As you implement steps to improve your school's trauma sensitivity, reevaluate and compare your scores. Any improvement, in any domain, indicates your school is heading in the right direction and is becoming more trauma-informed.

DOMAINS

Focus on Resilience (Step 1)

- Consider strengths.
- Assess students universal needs.

Awareness and Understanding (Step 2)

- Use of screening tool for trauma such as Life Events Checklist.

- Rather than diagnosing based upon behavior, school considers what is driving behavior.
- School provides trauma training to all staff.

Connections (Step 3)

- Adults make several attempts to connect with students.
- Peers/mentors are provided to every student.

Prioritizing Social and Emotional Skills (Step 4)

- Social and emotional skills are taught to students.
- Emotional awareness and regulation are taught and practiced with students.

Safety (Step 5)

- Working clocks.
- Visual cues.
- Adult supervision.

Play (Step 6)

- Play-based learning activities.
- Safe outside playground.
- Brain breaks.

Believe the Link Between Private Logic and Behavior (Step 7)

- School professionals understand how trauma impacts students' behavior and learning.
- Student strengths are always considered.
- Student's private logic is explored (how does student see themselves, interpret others and the world around them).

Partner with Families and Communities (Step 8)

- Family partnerships.
- Community collaborations.
- Mental health referrals.
- Community affairs committee.

Support Staff (Step 9)

- Staff breaks.
- Supervision.
- Professional development.
- Time off.
- Staff feedback.

Outcomes (Step 10)

- Data.
- School climate survey.

Other common universally collected school-based indicators like attendance, disciplinary data, and grades are important in an overall assessment system that is trauma-informed. When looking at this data, however, it should be done through a trauma-informed lens. For example, consider the cause of attendance patterns and ecological influences on behavior and academic performance.

In addition, trauma screening and assessment tools will help schools evaluate their students' exposure to trauma and toxic stress (e.g. ACE Questionnaire, Starr's *Life Events Checklist*) as well as their responses to their experiences (Starr's *Child and Adolescent Questionnaire*). When becoming trauma-informed, remember the importance of moving away from a deficiency-based approach, and toward a resilience-based approach. In addition to collecting only data that evaluates exposure, symptoms, and negative reactions, be sure to include measures that evaluate resilience factors (i.e., Resilience Quiz) and strengths such as coping style, self-efficacy, and affect regulation.

ACTIVITY:
Evaluation Tool Questionnaire

Request a *Trauma-Informed Schools Questionnaire* (re@starr.org) to understand where your school is measuring in its trauma-informed, resilience-focused journey.

Trauma-Informed Schools Questionnaire (TISQ)

The *Trauma-Informed Schools Questionnaire* (TISQ) measures school staff members' perceptions of the frequency to which they individually, and their school collectively, exhibit trauma-informed, resilience-focused knowledge and behaviors. Starr is in the process of testing the reliability and validity of this tool for its intended use. The Pre-TISQ is deployed as a baseline measure prior to intervention; a Benchmark-TISQ (B-TISQ) is deployed as a tracking measure for the trauma-informed, resilience-focused benchmarks achieved; finally, a Post-TISQ is deployed as a post measure after the interventions have been fully implemented. There are 10 TISQ subscales that make up the overall TISQ tool. Each subscale contains three statements measured by frequency from 1-5 (Never to Always), with each subscale average ranging from 1-5, and a total TISQ score average ranging from 1-5. Score ranges indicate whether a school is in its discovering, evolving, or flourishing phase of its trauma-informed, resilience-focused journey.

For the full TISQ tool, or to have Starr Commonwealth complete the analysis of your TISQ, please contact re@starr.org.

Snapshot of the TISQ*

CHECK ONE:

☐ Administrator ☐ Instructional ☐ Staff ☐ Non-Instructional Staff
☐ Other (specify) _____

INSTRUCTIONS:
Read each statement below and write the number that corresponds to the most appropriate answer in the box next to the statement.

ANSWERS:
1 - Never
2 - Once in a great while
3 - Some of the time
4 - Most of the time
5 - Always

Domain	Sample Question	Answer
FOCUS ON RESILIENCE	Most staff at my school practice strength-based approaches to classroom management (i.e., understand that behavior can be driven by unmet needs).	
AWARENESS & UNDERSTANDING OF TRAUMA AS AN EXPERIENCE	Most staff at my school approach interactions with students with an understanding of how trauma impacts the brain (i.e., emotions, behavior, and ability to learn).	
FOSTER CONNECTIONS	My school is intentional about making students feel connected to at least one person in the school setting (e.g., an adult or a peer).	
PRIORITIZE SOCIAL & EMOTIONAL SKILLS	My school models strategies to improve emotional regulation with students.	
EMOTIONAL & PHYSICAL SAFETY	My school has meaningful rules (e.g., encourages kindness, safety, and respect for all).	
PROMOTE PLAY	My school builds play-based activities into learning.	
BELIEVE IN THE LINK BETWEEN PRIVATE LOGIC & BEHAVIOR	My school considers how a student's view of "self" impacts their interactions.	
COLLABORATE WITH FAMILIES & COMMUNITIES	My school partners with families to make the school experience the best it can be for students.	
SUPPORT STAFF	My school supports staff with opportunities for self-care.	
COLLECT & SHARE OUTCOMES	My school uses trauma-informed, resilience-focused behavior support plans to assess the effectiveness of individual strategies with students.	

*This is a sample extract and not the full TISQ. For the full TISQ tool, or to have Starr Commonwealth complete the analysis of your TISQ, please contact re@starr.org.

Remember this...

- You can't see how far you have come if you don't know where you started.

Resilient School Project Patterns

STARR COMMONWEALTH
starr.org

Starr Commonwealth is a leader in healing trauma and building resilience in children and adolescents, training the professionals who serve them, and equipping all who care for them with tools to better understand and respond to their needs. Our Resilient Schools Projects embed professionals in school districts to teach students healthy social emotional skills and to work with educators to identify and reframe patterns of behavior to build resilience in kids.

There was a **50% decrease** in the number of **Office Discipline Referrals** after staff received training and committed to delivering trauma-informed, resilience-focused care.

After training staff to be trauma-informed, and resilience-focused, NWEA data reflected a majority of first and second graders were **meeting growth** in Reading and Math.

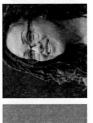

Increased Academic Engagement

Improved School Climate

Improved Student Behavior

Improved Teacher Morale

"Kids don't have to sit in rows quietly to learn. They need to move, they need fun, they may need a soothing tool, they need breaks."
—School Staff Member

The principal makes daily rounds throughout the building to check on the staff, which is helping build support and community with the staff.
—School Staff Member

90.3% of students agreed or strongly agreed that adults in their school **really care** about their students.

"I am more patient and curious about a student's behavior realizing a lot is not in their control at the moment."
—School Staff Member

"I'm calmer when dealing with student outbursts."
—School Staff Member

"Thinking about trauma when dealing with behavior [changed] my own problem solving behavior issues based on each student individually."
—School Staff Member

DRIVEN TO HEAL

Results are based on a case study of one school. Student survey results are based on 72 participants. Staff survey results are based on 16 participants.

Conclusion

We hope this resource provided you with not only an understanding of childhood trauma and how trauma can adversely influence learning, behavior, and relationships, but also specific tools you and your school will use to become a trauma-informed, resilient environment. All students need safe and supportive schools that can respond to an enormous body of research about how children's brains adapt to complex trauma and toxic stress.

Follow and use *10 Steps to Create a Trauma-Informed Resilient School,* along with its accompanying activities, worksheets, and evaluation tools with leadership, staff, students, parents, and even your board of education to guide both the creation and implementation of a trauma-informed, resilient school. Regardless of your role in education, you can help with the process of creating a trauma-informed classroom, school, and/or district. Educators can interrupt the impact of trauma and build resilience by creating a culture of awareness and sensitivity to each student's unique needs.

For more information on how we can help your school with training, consultation, or accreditation email info@starr.org.

Epilogue

The **10 Steps to Create a Trauma-Informed Resilient School** have become an integral component of Starr Commonwealth's flagship Resilient Schools Project — an evidence-informed and comprehensive systems approach to establishing a culture of resilience and trauma-informed practices in K-12 school buildings and districts nationwide. The goal of the project is to equip school professionals with knowledge, training, and support to foster resilience in children.

Starr's theory of change is that when trauma-informed and resilience-focused adults work within trauma-informed and resilience-focused systems, the wellbeing and success of children will increase. This theory is the foundation of the Resilient Schools Project that includes not only training, but also practical tools, coaching, and evaluation measures to implement and sustain trauma-informed, resilience-focused care in education settings. Read the Resilient Schools Project whitepaper (https://starr.org/resilient-schools-project-whitepaper/), which documents the many gains that meet the immediate needs of children.

Levin, S. S., Strand, G., & Ray, M. (2021). *The Resilient Schools Project: A systems approach to building trauma-informed, resilience-focused schools.* Albion, MI: Starr Commonwealth.

Resources

- Show this video clip at your next professional development:
  https://vimeo.com/181823590

- Take a Starr online course: https://starr.org/courses/

- Schedule a Starr Trauma-Informed Resilient Schools training at your school or district:
  Email info@starr.org or call 877.306.5256

- Purchase the *Life Events Checklist:* https://store.starr.org

- Purchase the *PTSD Evaluation Scale: Child and Adolescent Questionnaire:*
  https://store.starr.org

- Purchase the *Trauma-Informed, Resilience Focused Behavior Support Plan for Children and Adolescents:* https://store.starr.org

Learn more about school violence prevention

- CDC Division of Violence Prevention: www.cdc.gov/violenceprevention

- CDC Division of Adolescent and School Health: www.cdc.gov/healthyyouth/

- STRYVE: www.cdc.gove/violenceprevention/stryve/

- Stop Bullying: www.stopbullying.gov

- Surgeon General's Report on Youth Violence
  http://www.ncbi.nlm.nih.gov/books/NBK44294/

- Compliance with the Consumer Product Safety Commission's Playground Safety Handbook: http://www.cpsc.gov/CPSCPUB/PUBS/325.pdf

- Guide to Community Preventative Services: www.thecommunityguide.org/

References

American Academy of Pediatrics (2013). The crucial role of recess in school. *Pediatrics*, 131(1), 183-188.

Andersen, S., & Teicher, M. (2008). Stress, periods and maturational events in adolescent depression. *Trends in Neurosciences*, 31(4), 183-191.

American Psychiatric Association. (2013). *Diagnostic and statistical manual of mental disorders: DSM-5.* Washington, D.C: American Psychiatric Association.

Baroni, B., Day, A., Somers, C., Crosby, S & Pennefather, M. (2016). Use of the monarch room as an alternative to suspension in addressing school discipline issues among court-involved youth. *Urban Education,* 1-21.

Barr, J & Saltmarsh, S. (2014). It all comes down to leadership: The role of the school principal in fostering parent-school engagement. Educational Management Administration & Leadership 42(4):491-505

Beltman, S., Mansfield, C., & Price, A. (2011). Thriving not just surviving: a review of research on teacher resilience. *Educator Research Review,* 6, 185-207.

Briscoe-Smith, A & Hinshaw, S. (2006). Linkages between child abuse and attention deficit hyperactivity disorder in girls: Behavioral and social correlates. *Child Abuse and Neglect*, 30(11), 1239-1255.

Call, C., Purvis, K., Parris, S. & Cross, D. (2014). Creating trauma-informed classrooms. *Adoption Advocate,* 75.

Campbell, C., & Schwartz, D. (1996). Prevalence and impact of exposure to interpersonal violence among suburban and urban middle school students. *Pediatrics*, 98(3), 396-402.

Casella, R. (2003). Zero tolerance policy in schools: Rationale, consequences and alternatives. *Teachers College Record,* 105, 872-892.

Castro, M., Exposito-Casas, E. & Lopez-Martin, E. (2015). Parental involvement on student academic achievement: A meta-analysis. *Educational Research Review,* 14, 33-46.

Center on the Developing Child at Harvard University. (2007). A science-based framework for early childhood policy: Using evidence to improve outcomes in learning, behavior, and health for vulnerable children. Retrieved from *http://developingchild.harvard.edu/index.php/resources/ reports_and_working_papers/policy_framework/*

Chafouleas, S, Johnson, A., Overstreet, S. & Santos, N. (2016). Toward a blueprint for trauma-informed service delivery in schools. *School Mental Health*, 8:144-162.

Child Poverty in America (2017) retrieved 10/10/19 from childrensdefense.org/wp-content/ uploads/2018/09/Child-Poverty-in-America-2017-National-Fact-Sheet.pdf.

Cole, S., O'Brien, J, Gadd, M. Ristuccia, J. Wallace, D. & Gregory, M. (2005). *Helping traumatized children learn.* Boston, MA: Advocates for Children.

Felitti, V. (2009) Adverse Childhood Experiences and Adult Health. *Academic Pediatrics*, 9 (3), 131 - 132

Fox, D. & Olsen, L. (2014). *Home-School Relations.* Allyn & Bacon

Jones, S. M., & Bouffard, S. M. (2012). *Social and emotional learning in schools: From programs to strategies.* Social Policy Report, 26(4), Society for Research in Child Development.

Kyriacou, C. (2011). Teacher stress: Directions for future research. *Educational Review*, 53, 27-35.

Lobo, R., G. Brown, B. Maycock., A. McManus. 2010. Development of an evaluation framework and evaluation approaches for peer-based youth programs – Interim Report. Perth: Western Australian Centre for Health Promotion Research, Curtin Health Innovation Research Institute.

Mansfield, C., Beltman, S., Broadley, T., & Weatherby-Fell, N. (2016) Building resilience in teacher education: An evidenced informed framework. *Teacher and Teacher Education*, 54, 77-87.

National Child Traumatic Stress Network Schools Committee. (October 2008). Child Trauma Toolkit for Educators. Los Angeles, CA & Durham, NC: National Center for Child Traumatic Stress.

Prilleltensky, I., Neff, M. & Bessell, A. (2016). Teacher stress: what it is, why it's important, how it can be alleviated. *Theory into Practice,* 55: 104-111.

Ramstetter, C., Murray, R. & Garner, A. (2010). The crucial role of recess in schools. *Journal of School Health*. 80(11): 517-526.

Rice, K. F., & Groves, B. M. (2005). H*ope and healing: A caregiver's guide to helping your children affected by trauma.* Washington DC: Zero to Three Press.

Robert Wood Johnson Foundation (2007). *Recess Rules: Why the Undervalued Playtime May be America's Best Investment for Healthy Kids and Healthy Schools Report.* Princeton, NJ: Robert Wood Johnson Foundation. www.rwjf.org/files/research/sports4kidsrecessreport.pdf.

Saigh, P. & J. Bremner (Eds.) (1999). *Post-traumatic stress disorder: A comprehensive text,* Allyn & Bacon: New York.

Shonkoff, et al. (2012) Center on the Developing Child at Harvard University. Key concepts: toxic stress. http://developingchild.harvard.edu/topics/science_of_early_childhood/ toxic_stress_response.

Steele W., Raider, M. & Kuban, C. (2007) Connections, Continuity, Dignity, Opportunities: What allowed some to do better than others despite similar traumatic experiences. **School Social Work Journal.**

Stevenson, H. & Lee, S. Contexts of achievement: a study of American, Chinese, and Japanese children. *Monogr Soc Res Child Development,* 55(1-2): 1 – 123.

Substance Abuse and Mental Health Services Administration (2014). SAMHSA's Concept of Trauma and Guidance for a Trauma-Informed Approach. HHS Publication No. (SMA) 14-4884. Rockville, MD: Substance Abuse and Mental Health Services Administration.

U.S. Department of Education, Office for Civil Rights. (2014a, March). *Civil rights data collection data snapshot: Early childhood education* (Issue Brief No. 2). Retrieved from http://www2.ed.gov/about/offices/list/ocr/docs/crdc-early-learning-snapshot.pdf

Weinstein, D., Steffelbach, D. & Biassio, M. (2000). ADHD and PTSD Differential Diagnosis in sexually abused children. *Clinical Psych Review,* 20(3), 359-379.

Wilmott, R. (2008). The link between ADHD and child abuse. *Journal of Pediatrics,* 153(6), A3.

Wolpow, R., Johnson, M, Hertel, R. & Kincaid, S. (2009). *The heart of learning and teaching: Compassion, resiliency, and academic success.* Olympia, WA: Washington State Office of Superintendent of Public Instruction Compassionate Schools.

Zhang, A., Musu-Gillette, L., & Oudekerk, B., *Indicators of School Crime and Safety; 2015 (NCES 2016-079/NCJ 249758).* National Center for Education Statistics, U.S. Department of Education, and Bureau of Justice Statistics, Office of Justice Programs, U.S. Department of Justice. Washington, DC; 2016.

Zins, J., Weissberg, R., Wang, M., & Walberg, H. (2004). *Building academic success on social and emotional learning: What does the research say?* : Teachers College Pr.